I'll Let You Know

By the same Author

NINETEEN TO THE DOZEN
GIRLS WILL BE GIRLS
I SAY!

Edited by Arthur Marshall

NEW STATESMAN COMPETITIONS
SALOME, DEAR, *NOT* IN THE FRIDGE
NEVER RUB BOTTOMS WITH A PORCUPINE

ARTHUR MARSHALL

I'll Let You Know

MUSINGS FROM MYRTLEBANK

Illustrated by Tim Jaques

*'Asked his theme for a programme, Arthur Marshall said,
"I'll let you know".'*
    Radio Times, September 1980

HAMISH HAMILTON
London

First published in Great Britain 1981
by Hamish Hamilton Ltd
Garden House 57–59 Long Acre London WC2E 9JZ

British Library Cataloguing in Publication Data

Marshall, Arthur
  I'll let you know.
  1. English wit and humor
  I. Title
  828'.91407   PN6175
  ISBN 0-241-10644-3

Typeset by Rowland Phototypesetting Ltd
Printed in Great Britain by
St Edmundsbury Press, Bury St Edmunds, Suffolk

to
HAMISH HAMILTON
and
ROGER MACHELL
kind friends and encouragers
for so many years

Acknowledgements

Once more, I am grateful to the Editor of the *New Statesman* for his permission to reprint these pieces, all of which appeared originally in that magazine.

ARTHUR MARSHALL

Contents

Feeling My Way

Foreign restaurants abroad, still apparently just as anxious to help the currently impoverished and relatively rare English holidaying visitors as they would have been in the days long ago when the continent was permanently flooded with the British loudly demanding guides and Bath buns and foot-warmers and tea, are often given to providing menus in what they hope is an accurate and attractive English. I refuse to believe a friend who claims to have seen in Dieppe *fonds d'artichaut* diminished to 'chokebottoms', but who has not found *tarte maison* masquerading as 'house tart'? On a recent visit I made to Italy, the humble rabbit appeared on the menu more than once. I cannot imagine, and don't care to think, where it came from. The rocky and precipitous hills giving onto the western shores of the Gulf of Salerno would neither facilitate burrows nor feed their inhabitants. However, there available for lunch was stewed rabbit nestling among gravy and a mishmash of vegetables, the ensemble described triumphantly on the menu as 'Rubbit Huntsman Style'. Why the word 'rubbit' allied to 'huntsman' should make me instantly think of Lady Chatterley and her helpful gamekeeper friend I really cannot imagine.

I am not complaining but throughout my entire life nobody at any point has volunteered to provide me with any reliable and comprehensible sexual information of a sober and sensible kind. Nowadays the subject appears, if one can believe the newspapers, to rank in classroom importance with maths and geography, and with the age of the pupil ever decreasing. Soon they will be dragging toddlers from the sand-pit to show them what grown-ups can get up to when conditions are favourable. No such instruction occurred in my youth though I do recall a sort of half-hearted attempt at something in my last year at my prep school. We were in the top form and were being prepared in various ways for the wider world of the public school. The headmaster, a deaf, mahogany-faced Scotsman frequently full of

1

'It was heaven, just heaven'

whisky, relished the English language and was skilful at passing on his enthusiasm. But one morning he appeared to have temporarily abandoned Burns and *Julius Caesar* and had changed his line to, had we but known, that of fertilisation. I suppose there was some sort of preamble to prepare us for serious tidings of an intimate kind, but before we could even pause to wonder, we were in the very thick of it. The main flow of the narrative seemed to concern itself with what happened when two people 'loved' each other. 'This little thing provided by the male meets this little thing provided by the female in the female's cave and the little things link up and form a baby.'

Good gracious! What baffling stuff. We stared at each other non-plussed. One could, without much difficulty, identify and locate a 'little thing' about one's person, but could it be indeed this to which the headmaster had been referring? And if so, was not this frankness verging on the 'smutty talk' about which we had been so often warned? Indeed, a ribald section of us had already been in trouble over alleged 'smut'. When the tuneful hymn 'All Things Bright and Beautiful' came up, a popular favourite, in the church whose rear pews we graced for Matins every Sunday, some of us were found tampering with the text. 'Each little flower that opens, each little bird that sings', was all right, but on we bellowed with 'He made their gorgeous plumage, He made their tiny things.' 'Things' seemed to be more interesting than 'wings' but we were over-heard and a tremendous ticking-off followed. What would our parents think of us? We had ruined the service and desecrated the House of God (as it was partly composed of corrugated iron and was known to us as the Tin Tabernacle, it seemed as though God's housing plan had broken down). What a mercy that matron's shrill treble had deafened her to our filth. No bathing for a week.

Bathing, which took place from the uninviting and pebbly beaches and in the icy waters of the Solent, unexpectedly provided another small item to add to our limited knowledge of life's mysteries. It was widely known throughout the school that a rather jolly, youngish master called Sinclair ('Sink' to us) had become deeply enamoured of the local dentist's receptionist, a haughty beauty called Miss Bosford. They went walking together and he brought Miss Bosford, much done up, to one of the many school concerts. My friend Williamson claimed to have seen them at dusk locked in a deep embrace behind one of the odoriferous silos that dotted the landscape, but Williamson, a sunny character who liked things to go well, was known to embroider and by general agreement his information was discounted.

But was Williamson so wrong after all, for what was this exciting chat that a starry-eyed Mr Sinclair was pouring out one morning to those of us who sat happily at his table at breakfast? Besotted with Bosford, he was bursting to tell all, discretion thrown to the winds. A bathing picnic the night before. Moonlight. Sausage rolls. A bottle of wine. Miss Bosford, invited to take the water, had announced that she could not swim but added, doubtless proudly, that she could float. She had floated herself out from the shore and Mr Sinclair, positioned behind her and kicking away, had tugged her to and fro by the arms. It didn't sound all that much fun. 'But was it nice, sir?' we asked. 'It was heaven, just heaven,' he briefly replied, and fell silent. We munched on. All were aware that love was in the air and must be respected. But silence didn't prevent us from wondering, if Mr Sinclair and Miss Bosford truly loved one another, if little things were not this very moment joining up in Miss Bosford's cave, which would in due course cause her to abandon her promising career in dentistry.

3

Thoroughly flummoxed and inadequately equipped in this respect, I pressed on, hot for certainties and with my own physical scenery somewhat changed and embellished, to Oundle, a wholly admirable establishment in every way but at that time strangely shy about coming through with solid information about the subject under discussion. There was information but it was veiled, and there were inexplicable warnings and head-shakings. It seemed to me odd that love and sex, activities so highly praised in literature's pages, should seem to cause the greybeards such intense gloom and anxiety. Nobody at any point allowed that it was quite reasonably enjoyable. When the time for Confirmation came round, my fellow confirmands and I were addressed on Sunday evenings in the Chapel by the headmaster, a pleasant man but whose oratorical powers were limited. Full of supper, one dozed. But on one occasion I woke to find that we had left the sacraments and were back on a subject nearer home. 'You all know to what I am referring. You must all be on your guard, for this thing can wreck lives.' Oh dear. 'Thing' again. This is where I came in.

Such an Ordinary Person

One Spring day about 12 years ago I was approaching, as so often and so happily, the august and pleasing Piccadilly backwater of sets of chambers called Albany, invited to have lunch there with a kind friend. April showers were about and while I was crossing the courtyard a few drops of rain fell. Suddenly, as I got to the steps that lead up into the building, a bright vision appeared at the top of them, alone and splendidly perched up and visible, as though on a stage. Was she wearing pale lemon, or was it light grey and pink? Whatever it was, it caught, with the sweeping hat and white gloves, the eye. There was no mistaking the heavy, somewhat lop-sided face, the vast eyelids and the slightly petulant mouth of Dame Edith Evans. She then spoke, I suppose to an Albany porter hidden somewhere behind her, but it might have been London itself that she was addressing. 'I had thought of going out,' she said, 'but now I'm not so sure.' She made the very most of the sentence, giving the first six words a note of bright expectancy, and providing regret and disappointment for the last six. The phrases seemed to go on and hang suspended in the air for quite a time and there was what Enid Bagnold has described as 'a sort of silvery caress on a word here and there'. She hovered and she dithered and eventually she braved the raindrops, a modern Lady Bracknell off to snap up a few goodies at Fortnum's.

England and Turkey are, I suspect, the only countries where we admire our actresses more and more the older they become. Even with those gifted performers who sing and dance it has always been the same story – a gallant pressing on, singing away, until the last possible moment. Nobody thought it in any way odd that Miss Evans should tackle, so to speak, Rosalind at the age of 49, or Cleopatra at 58, though the latter performance did not find universal favour. A black American member of the cast, after watching her rehearse for some days, suddenly spoke his mind: 'Dat ole lady's goin' to lose us a lot of money.' He proved, alas, to be right on this occasion, but managements as a whole had, from the start of her blazing career, little cause to complain of idle box-offices.

The endless list of successes spanned 60 years – seasons at the Old Vic, her supreme Millament in *The Way of the World, Evensong, Robert's Wife, The Seagull,* dazzlements galore through *Waters of the Moon* to the triumph of *Daphne Laureola.* For all the brilliance and warmth of her acting, there was something strangely forbidding about her and it is therefore delightful to discover from the full and recently published biography how very funny she could be, whether discussing God ('I'm afraid I worry Him a bit') or refusing to play Lady Macbeth ('Don't think much of her') or travelling, either in India ('I went everywhere looking for a phallic symbol and I never saw a phallic anything. They must have disappeared when they saw me coming') or in Russia, where her method of coping with impossible Russian names was to call everybody Popov. She viewed unmoved the naked and tipsy bacchanalia in the film, *La Dolce Vita* ('I don't call *that* much of an orgy'), gave her opinion of stage nudity ('Mystery, that's what the theatre's all about and there's no mystery in a lot of goose-pimples') and cross-questioned the local vicar as to what might be expected in the after-life ('I don't want to meet a lot of unpleasant people like Queen Elizabeth. I'm quite sure she was unpleasant and I don't want to meet her').

'I think I'm such an ordinary person' she said, doubtless believing it for there was a weird mixture of humility and arrogance in her. She was, of course, no such thing and here, to reveal how very unordinary she was, is her own chosen biographer, Bryan Forbes, a loving and widely talented friend whom she bewitched at first sight and whom she instructed, giving him all the available documents and letters and papers, to tell nothing but the truth about her. This, in *Ned's Girl* (her father's friends, seeing her name on theatre posters, nudged each other and said 'That's Ned's girl'), he has faithfully done, and done with a skill and charm that make the book (Elm Tree Books will part with a copy for £5.95) required, and highly enjoyable reading, for all those who love the theatre.

All is fascination – the mixed background of a greatly loved GPO father and a mother who was the daughter of an illiterate cowman, the very skimpy education (she remained, in some ways, a bit of a goose), the spell in a London hat-shop, the evening classes in literature and Shakespeare run by a Miss Massey, who used to take the Streatham Town Hall and arrange

6

public performances by her students. After the meeting there with the famous William Poel (and *he* used to take the Ethical Church, Bayswater), Miss Evans abandoned millinery and, though never in the least stage-struck, wandered on to the professional stage by accident ('I think they thought this lump's got something in her'). She had indeed, but it was her custom modestly to attribute her achievements to God, with whom she enjoyed a nice working relationship ('You see, He never let me go on tour'). By not going on tour, she meant that she was never, early on, exposed to the danger of picking up from others cheap theatrical acting tricks. At first, her fellow performers were her equals until she speedily, acting and finding the way ahead with some extraordinary inborn instinct of her own, outstripped them. It mattered not at all that she was not beautiful ('I could *assume* beauty, and/did very often. My face took the paint well').

Success was immediate, and with fame came some of the tra-la-la that goes with it – she sat for portraits, judged a fashion competition for corselettes, posed for a *Tatler* photographer on the deck of the *Majestic* alongside George Arliss (they looked, says Mr Forbes, not unlike Ethel le Neve and Dr Crippen) and took part in charitable stage romps and mock trials, in one of which Peggy Ashcroft was sentenced to play Juliet for two years in Wigan with Wallace Beery as Romeo. She did some films, though her real triumphs in the cinema were, directed by her biographer, to come later ('I haven't got a film face. It moves about too much').

The sections that deal with her complex love affair and marriage are tactfully handled and extremely moving. He was Guy Booth, first of all a young ledger clerk in Woollands in Knightsbridge who, after the 1914 war, switched to the oilfields of Venezuela. There were long and painful separations and his letters (hers, alas, have perished) reveal how deep and lasting their love was. Many of them are reproduced here and, knowing how brief their marriage was (Guy died in 1935), they provoke lumps in the throat. There are other letters that one reads a good bit less emotionally, namely those from authors badgering her about this or that play (really, the way they go *on*), in particular the ageing Shaw whining away for years in the hope that she would play *The Millionairess* in London, a very doubtful theatrical treat which Hitler subsequently spared us.

It is altogether a book of great theatrical interest and import-ance and a model of its kind. A curious fact to tell you. When making my notes on the book before writing this piece, I see that I have nowhere taken the liberty of referring to the main subject of it as 'Edith'. I have put either 'Miss Evans' or 'Dame Edith'. Even in death she is formidable and somewhat unapproachable. 'Ordinary' my foot.

Speak as you Find

When, during the war, the Russians became, however involuntarily, our allies, the event was brought home to the nation and duly celebrated by various extremely English gatherings in London at, where else, the Albert Hall. The subject of one of these meetings was the rare bravery of the sailors who were operating the suicidal PQ convoys taking supplies to our hard-pressed snowy friends across the dangerous northern seas. It was felt important to make it clear to the audience from the start how very *cold* Russia was and to this end the lights came up on Ralph Richardson, perched on a sort of plinth and wearing whitish grey robes indicating chill, with Sybil Thorndike on another plinth in matching attire. Sir Ralph spoke first. 'Twenty below, thirty below, forty below,' he intoned, striking a suitably icy note, upon which Dame Sybil inflated those splendid lungs and echoed these temperature readings with an impressive '. . . and slowly flows Wolga.' The beloved lady, ever diligent, had evidently discovered that in spoken Russian the Volga comes out as the 'Wolga' (does it?). After further scene-setting jabber, there was a good bit of music and of marching about by merchant seamen with the tops of their sea-boots turned down, after which we all dutifully subscribed £1 to something or other and then went home to our dried egg and the last of the margarine.

On another occasion, they brought over a Russian delegation which included the famous Russian lady sniper who had already, operating alone on the steppes, bagged 89 Germans and was thirsting for more, a commanding uniformed figure called Ludmila something. The British public, who had been having bombs dropped on them for two years, already knew about war and were inclined to treat the occasion lightly. A female rifle woman seemed to them all that was most hilarious, and on her appearance, accompanied by an interpreter, there were merry cries of 'Look out, 'ere she comes. Duck, everybody! Mind yer heads!' The Russians were, rightly, not amused; the interpreter

9

advanced. 'Ludmila say, war no joke.' Eventually, after some country dancing displays by women's institutes, the doughty markswoman was presented with a silver tea-pot and a set of Dickens, tastefully morocco-bound and handsomely tooled. The recipient looked, as well she might, nonplussed ('Ludmila say, good afternoon'). Throughout the proceedings not one smile had anywhere been visible on a Russian face. It was all gloom and doom. Could these people be, we wondered, true representatives of Shangri-la, the imagined heaven of the far Left and Communist sympathisers who flourished intellectually in the Twenties and Thirties, and who nowadays grace, here and there, the shop-floor?

'Do you know what the dead do in heaven?' cries an anguished character in Clemence Dane's *A Bill of Divorcement*. 'They sit on their golden chairs and sicken for home.' The plight of the voluntary exile, if such one may call a traitor, is explored in Alan Bennett's thoughtful new play, *The Old Country*, and at least we know, from personal accounts, what was the fate of Guy Burgess. His usefulness long since exhausted, he sat on his golden chair swigging vodka (?wodka), wearing an Old Etonian bow tie, playing on a portable gramophone a not very good Jack Buchanan record, with the tears streaming down his face. He was, however, responsible for a remarkable display of loyalty by a delightful lady that I knew, a Miss Warren.

The quality of loyalty, of which Miss Warren was once to give such a fine example, is strange, for however misapplied or disastrously pursued a loyalty it may be, it is impossible to have anything but admiration for it. Not even those who tend to sneer at all human virtues can make any sort of headway against loyalty. Some years ago, Miss Warren was cashier in the dining-room (known to us as the 'coffee-room') of the London club of which I am happily a member. After munching one's selected goodies down, it was to her that one went to pay up, passing the time of day as one did so. She sat high up at a sort of raised desk, viewing the landscape o'er, and gave the impression of being seated on a throne. Her manner was indeed both regal and affable, but one wouldn't have cared to get on the wrong side of her. At this time, another member of the club was Guy Burgess. He liked, as I did, Miss Warren, and they would exchange jokes. He had considerable natural charm and his manners towards everybody in the club, whether employees or fellow members, were impeccable, a pleasant trait that is not always present among those who frequent clubs. He took, for whatever reason, a

The doughty markswoman was presented with a silver teapot

lively interest in people as such, and was entirely lacking in egocentricity.

When the Burgess and Maclean scandal broke, the club rooms buzzed with chat. Voices, raised or lowered, boomed or muttered their uninformed views. Know-alls wagged their dreary heads and hindsight was everywhere ('Never trusted the fellow . . .'). A group of members, waiting to pay their lunch bills at the cash desk, were loudly discussing the affair and were uniformly hot in condemnation. They rattled on and on until they suddenly became aware of a Presence. It was Miss Warren who had put down her pen and had risen to her feet and was now towering even higher above them, a huge avenging angel. An alarmed silence fell and then Miss Warren spoke, and in a voice that, trembling with rage, echoed round the coffee-room. 'I don't care what anybody else says about Mr Burgess, he has always been extremely kind to *me*. If you want to know what people are really like, ask the club servants. They know who's truly nice and who isn't. Mr Burgess is a very nice man, *much nicer than many members I could name*.' Her furious glance swept the little group beneath her, picking out a bald head here, a pair of gleaming pincenez there. Terrified, they hurriedly paid their bills and slunk humbled away. By the time my turn came to pay, she was herself again. 'How's Devon? We haven't seen you for quite a time. That saddle of mutton looked tasty. That will be eighteen shillings exactly.' I could have hugged her.

I feel that I should be letting Miss Warren (now dead, alas) down if I did not state now, as I was not shy of stating then, that I was a friend of Guy's. We had been at Cambridge together and he, artistically gifted, had designed sets for plays in which I had acted. He led a university life that was a good bit faster than mine. Indeed, he had an M.G. car and his rooms in Trinity, and later in London, were a confused mass of rumpled Old Etonian ties, stale bits of cake, tins of jellied eels, half-burnt lamp-shades, gramophone records of all descriptions (he particularly enjoyed the horror of 'laughing songs'), and innumerable bottles of Cointreau from which friends were encouraged to sip, no matter how early or advanced the hour. There was a sort of mini-spinet on which he occasionally twanged a melody and in the plugless bath the water was kept in by the suction supplied by an old tennis ball enshrouded in an old tennis sock that had not recently made contact with soap and water destined for itself alone.

He was generous and carefree and it really didn't seem to matter much that his ears were sometimes rather grubby. He was as bright as a button and he could be extremely funny. He found out one day that I had never read Dickens. I explained that my father, a passionate admirer who seldom read anything else, had attempted, with the best intentions, to make me read him too and of course I had violently rebelled. One evening at the club, Guy read me, in a richly comical voice, the Mrs Gamp sections from *Martin Chuzzlewit*, and my laughter was so violent and uncontrolled that we had to stop. This is the kind of thing for which one will be grateful all one's life.

It is, I suppose, the selflessness and unprofitability of an unquestioning loyalty such as Miss Warren's that make it such an unassailable virtue. Other virtuous excellences, among them zeal, patience, honesty, dutifulness and industry, all tend to get you somewhere (a cherished seat on the board: that bank managership: a job at the Mint) but loyalty really leads nowhere. Cordelia was reviled and disinherited by her dotty old dad and led a short life that few would envy. Nancy's devotion to Bill Sykes can hardly be said to have benefited her career, and the boy stood on the burning deck (whence all but he had fled) to very little personal advantage save that of a brief appearance in an extremely hackneyed poem.

Without Tears

For examples of lethargy, idleness and general hopelessness one can hardly beat the British. London must be the only city in the world where wartime bomb damage is still plainly visible. I am referring to what is left of the façade of the Shaftesbury Theatre in Shaftesbury Avenue, the real one I mean (the theatre that now calls itself by this name should properly be The Princes). The ruins of the old Shaftesbury seem now to be partly a fire station and partly a car park. I understood that there was an agreement that all our theatres were to be preserved and their number in no way diminished. Why then has nothing been done in the way of rebuilding this charming house? It made a delightful home for the plays of Frederick Lonsdale and others.

When wandering in nostalgic mood through London's theatreland, I sometimes long for a magic wand with which to restore past glories to each theatre as I go by it. My somewhat old-fashioned tastes are at once revealed. At the London Pavilion, which has no right to be a cinema, there would be a Cochran revue by Noël Coward. At Her Majesty's, an enchanting musical called *Music in the Air* (Jerome Kern, and the best composer of them all). At the Criterion, Marie Tempest in no matter what. And at the Globe there would be *While the Sun Shines*, at the Phoenix, *The Browning Version*, at the Duchess, *The Deep Blue Sea*, at the Lyric, *Love in Idleness* – all of them plays, I need hardly tell you, by Terence Rattigan.

I first met him in 1938 at a birthday party of Ivor Novello's in that famous Aldwych flat perched high up above the Strand Theatre. Guests ascended to it in a lift about as capacious as a twin-berthed coffin and in which, in sardine-tin intimacy, one always found oneself pressed up against and nose to nose with somebody surprising like Gladys Cooper or Tallulah Bankhead. It would have seemed both priggish and unchummy to have gone rattling up back to back. You may well wonder what I, a humble public schoolmaster (£250 a year, with free laundry and the run of

14

'Munch it up, dear, you're all skin and bone'

my teeth), was doing there, so theatrically and socially out of my depth. A brisk explanation. I had recently made, for Columbia, some allegedly funny gramophone records which had, remarkably, found particular favour with the acting profession, Ivor especially, and I was there to spout them out to his assembled friends after supper.

I was, naturally, inarticulate with nerves but Terry Rattigan, his charm and good manners instantly apparent, was a great support ('I'll laugh, anyway'). *French Without Tears* was in the middle of its triumphant run but he was entirely modest and did not look in any way like a successful playwright. But then, what ought a playwright, successful or not, to look like? A timorous householder, opening his front door to an Identikit amalgam of the salient features of Barrie, Shaw, Ibsen, Galsworthy and Pinero, might at once have taken fright and put up the chain ('Not today, thank you'). Terry, as slim and as neat and as what fashion writers will call 'well groomed' as he was to remain for most of his life, might have been somebody from Lloyd's perhaps, or from an ancient and highly respected City firm of wineshippers. He had been an opening bat for the Harrow First XI and the aura of cricket never quite left him. We were of an age and, though he had by

15

then met the world, he was still as stagestruck as I and together we goggled at the splendid creatures before us – Zena Dare, Beatrice Lillie, Dorothy Dickson, Leslie Henson and almost every other star then in London. There was also an up-and-coming couple, who had just fallen desperately in love with each other, and their names were Laurence Olivier and Vivien Leigh. My ordeal, when it came, was far less alarming than might be imagined. Theatre people are very kind and make the best audience in the world.

Somerset Maughan, himself too a happy recipient of overnight dramatic success, had a word to say about its effect on the author of *French Without Tears*. 'He'll make a great deal of m-m-money, and in two years time he won't have a p-p-penny of it left.' This was partly true, mainly because of Terry's generosity. He was, in every sense, a giver, and the subsequent dazzling stream of Rattigan successes enabled him increasingly to give more. He had a passion for owning houses and for filling them with his friends. There have been houses in Sonning and Sunningdale, in Ischia and Bermuda, in Wentworth, Brighton, Eaton Square and Bonnie Scotland, and with the houses there sometimes went rather strange servants whose domestic oddities often pleased their master. At lunch, a distinguished actress, as it might be Diana Wynyard, or possibly Margaret Leighton, spoon poised above the vegetable dish that was being handed to her by a friendly but rum butler and trying to decide just how many of the courgettes to scoop out on to her plate, would find her meditations interrupted by an urgent hiss (''urry up, dear, I haven't got all day'). Or, even more agitating, a cascade of brussels sprouts would come flying over her shoulder in the general direction of her plate, followed by a large dollop of unwanted mashed potato ('Munch it up, dear, you're all skin and bone'). Terry would never have dreamt of trying to 'correct' such unconventional behaviour. He would have considered it impertinent. Human beings were what they were and you must take them as you find them, merely noting down their idiosyncracies for possible future use. Human beings fascinated him and he was extremely gregarious. In every respect but one he really preferred, I think, the company of women. And in that one respect, he was never a victim of the promiscuous urges that afflict so many wonky gentlemen. His loves were for life.

And how tremendously be liked to laugh. The occasions were frequent. On a Berkshire golf-course an unliterary colonel approached him knowingly with 'I say, aren't you that writer chap-pie? *French Without Leave,* eh? Where on earth do you writer chappies get your ideas from?' Then there was a female medium who insisted on coming to visit him in his Sonning house and who, once inside the door, fainted dead away with a loud shriek ('Mr Rattigan, you've got something very nasty in your hall'). There was the time when signing a foreign hotel register somewhat indistinctly, and possibly a little tipsily, he later appeared in the *Continental Daily Mail* as 'Recently arrived at the Hotel Crillon: Mrs T. Rothbun.' There was the evening when, living at that time in Albany, he had invited a famous mimic friend to dine who, on leaving at midnight, had loudly 'done' Edith Evans, another resident, the sounds reaching the ears of the then secretary and considerably agitating him ('Excuse me, Mr Rattigan, but does Miss Evans *drink?*'). And he never ceased to enjoy the memory of a manacled female Houdini, 'the under-water escapologist' once seen at a fair and whose barker's phrase he himself always used when about to enter a swimming-pool ('Ladies and Gentlemen, Madame Aqua will now lower herself into the tank').

The recent BBC TV 'tribute' to him was made, I understand, about a year ago and with his full cooperation. He can hardly have known that it would be used as an obituary. Most of the other obituary notices that have appeared about him seem to me to have been less than generous. Grudging, they were. They certainly covered the ground but with little hint that here was a quite exceptional talent and a warm humanity, no suggestion that the plays were masterpieces of dramatic construction. Few writers thought to mention the enormous pleasure they have brought, and still bring. I do see that, to those also involved in the theatre, the huge success was hard to bear. His aims were simple and remained the same – to please. He wrote in these very pages about Aunt Edna, the mythical middle-brow theatre-goer (she had recently been to see the rather unacceptable *Waiting for Godot* and was airing her views). Aunt Edna is still, with her male counterpart, the backbone of the British theatre public (well, just look about you next time you go). The progressive theatre of ideas was not for her. She did not care for 'messages'. Other dramatists have managed quite well without them. *Hamlet* is quite an effective piece, but the only possible message to be extracted from it is that it doesn't always pay to take an after-lunch nap in an orchard.

The autobiography which he never wrote was to have been called *Without Tears,* a suitable summing-up of a happy life but inapplicable to the many friends and admirers who now mourn him.

Maids of Honour

During the war, and passing in uniform through a succession of officers' messes on my way up the military ladder to a rather doubtfully useful stardom as a Lt.-Col. in the Intelligence Corps, I always had a lurking fear that some evening, after dinner and during ha-ha-ha-time over the port, I should be required, by bluff old Brigadier Bimbo, to produce a dirty joke. It was not prudishness that worried me but the fact that I knew none. It is always assumed that anybody who is connected, however distantly, with the world of entertainment, has a merry fund of such tales at command. This is not correct. The only things of the sort that I could ever remember were entirely feeble and muddled riddles ('Why did Sir Adrian Boult?' 'Because he saw the salad dressing'), and I knew better than to parade such milk-and-water stuff before moustachioed Majors. But as it turned out, jokes of a lewd kind, and the tellers of them, were not much in demand. It is understandable, yet somehow strange, that war and privation and danger should prove such a stimulus to enjoyment of the rather better sort of printed word. After dinner, and when not actively giving old Jerry what for, all ranks tended to retire quietly to bed and tuck in to books by, say, Arnold Bennett or Hardy or Wells. Poetry too was in great demand. Reading of any kind was a solace.

As a matter of fact, I rather enjoy riddles, good or bad as the case may be. The late (and with what sadness I write that word) Paul Dehn had a similar liking, though the riddles that he himself invented were always in the topmost class. In quoting one of them now, and a rather saucy one, I must emphasise that Paul and I, both nurtured at excellent schools (Shrewsbury and Oundle) and reputable universities (Oxford and Cambridge), had been made, and remained, well aware of the dangers of 'smutty talk' and did not at all go in for it. But literature, even the best, requires every now and then a strong and pivotal word to lend it point, and you will find a not very shocking one in the riddle which follows, together with an archaic English usage still popular in those brainteasers that, with paper hats and musical instruments, come tumbling out of Christmas crackers. Ready? 'What is the difference between a debutante and an Elizabethan gallant who hath split his cod-piece?' Answer: 'There is no difference. They both have coming-out balls.'

No longer true (of debutantes, anyway). You cannot, as the former Henrietta ('Deb of the Year') Tiarks explains, spend evenings in discotheques, put on make-up, smoke and go out with boyfriends from about the age of 15 on, and then 'come out'. There is nothing left to come out from. There can be few people, and certainly not the girls themselves, who regret the disappearance of formal presentations at Court. Least regretful of all must be the Queen herself (the constant bobbing up and down in front of her of hundreds of white visions, with swaying plumes, was said to have brought on such severe sea-sickness that she had to raise her sights and just stare swimmingly at the wall above their heads). Nobody liked to be smiled at by the Duke of Edinburgh. Kindness itself, he reserved his beams for the ugly ones to cheer them up. In my youth, these English roses were to be seen constantly in the illustrated papers and magazines during the 'season'. I remember a particularly engaging one called Primrose Salt, a name which to those interested in cooking seems to suggest an exciting new herbal additive, just the thing to have handy when called upon to 'adjust your seasonings'.

Margaret Pringle deals in *Dance Little Ladies* (Orbis: £6.75 and very lavishly illustrated) with the acute and age-old problem for parents of how on earth to get rid of their daughters (the popular and well-tried method of just leaving them out on a lofty rock is no longer legal). The public social exposure in the 'presentation' system, invented by upper-crust Victorians with too much time on their hands, maintained itself, despite wars, depressions, strikes and the briskly changing social scene, until 1957 and seems now, as it did to some then, idiotic and wasteful beyond belief. The numbers alone are staggering. In the 22 years up to 1957, 53,000 debutantes, virginal (elaborate sex was right out), apprehensive (though their curtseys were expertly Vacani-taught, it was only too easy to measure your length before the monarch), their puppy-fat squeezed into, for many, totally unsuitable and wildly expensive dresses, presented by a titled relation or somebody bought for hard cash (the going rate for Duchesses was around £2,000 a time), glided jerkily before their sovereign in the grand mass cattle market. The war years meant

19

that there were 20,000 carcases queuing up for the treat, though by then fringe lunacies, such as instruction at a Kensington school of deportment in the correct way for ladies to pick up dropped handkerchiefs (bottoms as near the ground as possible in a sort of mini-curtsey, but watch that skirt!) had ceased.

And for whom was all this trouble being taken? Who were the handsome Adonises, who the knights in shining armour come eagerly to claim their dazzling prize? 'Oh God', used to mutter, as the front door bell rang, the father of one debutante as she waited, all togged up for a ball, for her escort, 'here comes another bounder!' They were known as 'deb's delights' and here, from an unusual source, is a description of them: 'The kind of men one meets at these functions are insufferable. They are immature, arrogant, insensitive, callous and unbelievably stupid. Guards officers, trainees at Lloyd's, aspiring stock-brokers – chinless juveniles one year out of public school, living in Chelsea or Kensington on small allowances from home.'

The views of our informant (from, surprisingly perhaps, our NS itself) are borne out on all sides, especially by the 'delights' themselves. Appalling behaviour in famous London houses was the thing and everybody *roared*. 'One was frightfully rude. People behaved as they imagined people did in *Vile Bodies*. I remember one night when we were meant to be on guard at St. James's Palace. One of us got absolutely soaked and when he got to Marlborough House, where Queen Mary lived, he halted the troop and started to throw gravel at the window and shouted out that she was an old Hun.' Queen Mary, needless to say, behaved impeccably, even interceding with the Colonel on behalf of the culprit (confined to barracks for a month).

A final surprise, and again from the NS. Those who haven't, perhaps, rated us very highly socially must think again. 'In 1956 the NEW STATESMAN threw a cocktail party at Londonderry House for 450 guests and the bill was £604 7s 7d. Among other things, the guests consumed 25 bottles of gin, 12 bottles of whisky and 168 bottles of non-vintage Moët et Chandon at 26s. 6d. a bottle. Cigarettes were provided free.' I remember it well, and very nice too. Those were the days.

Here We Go Again

Foreign visitors to our shores, no longer a purely seasonal phenomenon but, like cucumbers and globe artichokes and pineapples, now so fully available on every day of the year that one sometimes tires of them, find themselves faced in London by various perplexities. For example, there is the fact, to which the permanent residents are now sadly accustomed, that the most popular numbered motor buses travel along, at half-hourly intervals, in a communally self-protective pack like wildebeests, nose to tail in clutches of five (I once saw eight No 14s, queen of buses, jammed together in Shaftesbury Avenue at 2.25 p.m., but perhaps they were returning from a reunion lunch at a chic Soho pizza parlour, or were on their way to a matinée). There is also the fact that, unless humans open their mouths to speak, it is no longer possible to tell, from the clothes they are wearing, which person is what. A camouflage of general subfusc and dirty-jeaned drabness covers everybody and we merge into the background. The French, tremendous snobs despite that rather showy and ostentatious Revolution, are for ever peering about for *les milords anglais* whom they still imagine to be bowling along in their Rolls and shrieking insults ('Cow!' 'Villain!') at the chauffeur down a gold-plated speaking-tube, little realising that that shifty, down-at-heels creature beside them in the bus queue is either a *milord* or just a lord, off to pocket his daily attendance fee at the House.

Then there is the question of surnames. Although brought up in their foreign schools and led, in their English language lessons, to think that every other British person is called either Smith or Brown (*'Que fait Madame Smith?'* 'She is steaming her pudding'. *'Was macht Frau Brown?'* 'She is making jokes and laughing "Ho ho" '), the evidence of their eyes on hoardings and walls, on the backs of bus seats and chalked on pavements, tells them otherwise. I am speaking, of course, of the extensive Wanks family, ever anxious to leave behind them proof that they, or one of their close friends, has been present. On entering an underground station, it is in no way surprising to see, scratched up in the passage-way that leads trackwards, the proud names of Les Wanks, Stan Wanks and Rod Wanks. Sometimes just initials are used – P. H. Wanks, N. R. Wanks. Occasionally there is a generous measure of admiration and praise for the entire, and predominately male, family ('There's nothing like a few good Wanks'). Once again, the poor Frogs find themselves baffled ('*Qui sont ces Wanks?*'). The bearers of this name are, I incline to think, not from the upper-crust and they tend to favour shortened Christian names with rather a lower-crust lilt to them – Len, Perce, Sid. I have yet to see any mention of Peregrine Wanks, Jocelyn Wanks or Osbert Wanks. Perhaps I don't go to the right walls.

There is one perplexity which will not at once offer itself as such to foreign visitors. To be aware of it one needs to have been frequently resident in the capital. It concerns pigeons. In the thousands of miles that I have walked and hours that I have spent and years that I have lived in London, I have never once seen a *dead* pigeon, apart from those served up on a plate, partly disguised by *les légumes* and masquerading as *poulet*, in wartime restaurants. But among the millions of pigeons that exist in London, many thousands must daily die. Where, then, do they do it? Certainly not on streets or pavements, nor do they come plopping lifelessly out of the sky onto one's nut. Have they I wonder, like elephants, some secret, secluded haunt (screened off section of the Mansion House roof? A disused ventilator shaft at what was dear old Pontings?) known to them all and to which, at the approach of the dread hour, they flap and, in messy roof-top confusion, turn up their pigeon toes? And what then, there being no vultures (none with wings, anyhow) hereabouts to tidy them up and pick the bones clean?

I peered about for dead pigeons (no dice) on my way through St James's Park, bound for St James's Palace to see, on view as I write, the representative display of gifts lavished on the Queen at her jolly Silver Jubilee. Well aware that many NS readers are territorially denied these treats, I bring from time to time, as you know, news of such matters, in this case in fuller detail than in a recent reference in these pages and for those who missed BBC-2's guided tour. Here again are perplexities galore for foreigners (the queue was stiff with them) who, from some of the gifts, will form a very odd view of Her Majesty's activities. What, for example, does she get up to with a necklace made of teeth, a cowhide (which I take to be the outside of a dead cow rather than a nature-lover's foliage-bedecked Wendyhouse from which secretly to observe cows), and a membership badge of a Welsh Trampoline Club (can there be a Palace rumpus-room with the sovereign bouncing healthfully up and down?). Then what can overseas visitors, not to speak of ourselves or the recipient herself, possibly make of two miniature chairs fashioned from tin cans, a red, white and blue felt donkey, a tinsel sash, an 18th-century pewter syringe ('This may hurt you a little'), a carving of two Maoris kissing and a large sago pot?

Members of the royal family clearly have very little time for reading, even if their inclinations actually led that way, and therefore, as the donors obviously realised, almost any book comes as a delightful novelty. One can picture the unfamiliar objects being passed excitedly from hand to hand at breakfast, and striking passages read out. Certain of the volumes presented lend themselves admirably to this treatment – *History of Sidcup Cricket Club, Caring for Textiles* and *East Gwilliambury in the 19th Century.* Purely visual pleasures have not been neglected and photographs and paintings have come pouring in. During that spare five minutes before the next Ambassador presents his credentials (and whatever can they be? Do they ever forget them? '*Where* are your credentials?'), Her Majesty can feast her eyes on Sherwood Forest, an oil platform, the Ilfracombe Corps of Drums, Stockton-on-Tees, 'a picture of two people reading *The Times*' and Queen Victoria done in needlework.

One item I at first found very worrying, 'a Greetings telegram in stainless steel'. Could this be some new Post Office wheeze to bump up the already outrageous price ('We also have them in burnished gold'), or a clever method of preventing them being blown away at the front door as you sign for them, in which case telegrams made of lead might be even better? However, I now see that this extremely unusual gift comes from the Lord Mayor and Citizens of Sheffield, clearly advertising home products. Another item that I don't quite follow comes from Members of the Diplomatic Corps, who decided to hand over 'a dinner table' (something to put that sago pot on at last). How has the Queen been managing hitherto, one wonders? Plastic telly-trays perched on her knees? Indeed, there are indications that when donors decided to club together, they rather lose their heads – the people of Newfoundland (a book containing 300,000 signatures), the Shell Co. Ltd (snaps of fireworks), the California Historical Society ('a printed resolution').

What anxious discussions as to a suitable present went on, I ask myself, in the Vatican? I was once in St Peter's Square on Easter Day and got blessed, along with a million others, by the Pope. He appeared to us high up at a very non-grand window that looked to belong to a housemaid's bedroom. One almost expected to see long black stockings hanging out to dry. It was a pleasing little ceremony and one that our Archbishop, the clergy being so woefully uncolourful, might well copy from some attic window in Lambeth Palace. His Holiness seemed a delightfully simple, modest personality and his gift to the Queen is in keeping with it. Just a bible: and a secondhand one at that.

By Royal Appointment

Although I have in this column liberated from time to time, in loyal answer to loyal readers' requests, a few minor details of my private life (just a word here and a name there concerning my commodious habitat and my village world), nobody respects more than I the sanctity of privacy and the need to preserve it, a need that in this joyous Jubilee year 1977 must surely be felt more than ever by the very highest in the land. It is partly for this reason that I am abandoning my daring plan, inspired by a very natural curiosity, of shinning over that wall, pressing my nose to the Palace windows and having a good dekko at what they are all munching for breakfast. But the true reason really is that I no longer need to go to all that trouble to find out. I now *know*.

My information comes from, of all the unlikely sources to be in any way connected with kippers and kedgeree and bacon and eggs, the pages of *Debrett*. Within, for all to see who can gain access to this august publication, sits an alphabetical list of Royal Warrant Holders, a list based, as it announces in the edition I have seen, on the names published in the *London Gazette* of 1 January 1975. Here are to be found in fact the names, some famous (Fortnum), some obscure (Mrs J. Lightbody), of all the purveyors and suppliers and providers of life's necessities who keep the royal family going in the way of nourishment and clothes and cars and creature comforts and so on.

Not that the royal family is for this purpose lumped together in a conglomerate. Naturally, some like this and some like that. Identification marks alongside the suppliers' names indicate whether this or that goody goes to Her Majesty, or to the Queen Mother, or to both of them (as pretty often occurs), or solely to the Duke of Edinburgh. And at last we know exactly what goes on and who gets what. One or two nostalgic marks apply only to departed monarchs – Georve VI, Edward VIII and George V. Maybe diligent research in back numbers could show one where dear Queen Mary used down the years to acquire her unforgettable toques (her gracious bowing, from the back seat of large motor-cars, was so regular and unvaried and clockwork-like that a rumour went about that she was in actual fact enjoying a pleasant doze and was being worked off the back-axle).

Armed with this information and the list of names, what more agreeable pastime can there be than to picture the start of an ordinary day at Buckingham Palace? Dawn, with the birds happily twittering in the garden, and at 7.30 a.m. the Queen stirs in her sleep and, awaking to an Airwick-fresh bedroom, switches off the Chubb Intruder Alarm, rises from the warm embrace of her Sleepeezee bedding, dons her mules, pauses for a moment to admire the hygienic wizardries of Jeyes Fluid and Sanitas (of Sanitas House SW9) and then it's into that hot tub, with generous spongefuls of Pears' creamy suds and, at the ready in case of a watery accident, her Beaufort Air-Sea Life Saving Equipment. A hearty towelling down and then comes the supportive comfort of the best handiwork of Rigby & Peller (corsetières), topped by a deceptively simple day-dress from Hartnell, firmly marked with Cash's Name Tapes just in case there's a muddle at the laundry.

Then, hoping that the Express Dairy has called (as promised), it's downstairs, with the cosy whirr of the Electrolux Suction Cleaner humming away, an admiring glance at the half-dozen new organ blowers standing crated in the hall and just delivered by Messrs Watkins and Watson of Wareham (they will be handy as Christmas presents), a quick dash to Day & Hewitt's Animal Medicines cupboard for a swift purgative for the corgis, and then into the breakfast room where a super spread awaits. There are Cooper's marmalade, Harris's bacon, the full range of Heinz in all its nutritious glory, Quaker oats, preserves from Tiptree, Angostura Aromatic Bitters, Kellogg's assorted cereals, Lucozade, tempting kippers from Associated Fisheries (Neptune House, Bermondsey), fragrant herrings from MacFisheries (Ocean House, Bracknell), Baxter's pork sausages (slosh on the Colman's, there's bags more in the larder), Aylesbury Mushrooms, cascades of Cerebos (from Cerebos House, Willesden), and, standing ready in the corner, one of Berkel & Parnall's Slicing Machines, just in case any of the viands need slicing. Then, with the meal over, the Cross's Disposable Tableware is gathered up, loaded into one of Cartem's Sack Holders, popped into plastic refuse luxibins and then, presumably, disposed of. And, on the very tick of nine, work begins, with the Venus pencils and the Parker pens flying over the embossed writing paper and Her Majesty's Addressograph machine clanks merrily into action.

Over in Clarence House, a roughly similar picture presents itself but with subtle differences. Here there is less sense of urgency. The Queen Mother rises, I rather suspect, a pinch later (and who could blame her, nestling as she is in the downy arms of Slumberland?) and, after a lavish going-over with Morny soap, a testing choice of corsetières lies before her: shall it be the Woodward-Yorke or the Madame Marcyle of WC1? Meanwhile, downstairs in the kitchen regions, the 'Scotchbrite' scouring pads

All the purveyors and suppliers and providers of life's necessities who keep the royal family going

27

have been violently at work preparing pots and pans and dishes for the bewildering flood of tuck that's been daily pouring in through the back door. No quinquireme of Nineveh ever came from further afield or was more heavily laden on arrival – cheese from the Orkneys and Jermyn Street, biscuits from Blackpool, Musk's sausages from Newmarket, Emmett's pickled hams from Suffolk, cream (and is it wise?) from United Dairies, Baxter's Scottish Specialities (baps, would you think?), Chivers' Christmas puddings from Cambridge, Rowntree's table jellies, Wall's meat pies, almonds from Mitcham, Weetabix, Antony's Tudor Queen tongues, joints from Staines, shoulders from Eaton Square, Floris pâtisserie, Findus frozen peas, and fruit from Aberdeen. And what a sweet tooth we do seem to have. There's the full Nestlé range, cocoa and chocolate from Bournville itself, Ackermann's chocs from the Finchley Road, and Sharp's toffees (from Kreemy Works, Maidstone).

A contented sigh, a gentle dabbing of the fingers, and then it's out with the Aquascutum, on with the peaches and cream (Elizabeth Arden), into the Daimler and off, with that enchanting smile, to open something or pat a horse and delight everybody. Digestion pills are not mentioned and no credit is given but they must surely exist and have been swallowed and even now are completing their beneficial work within.

By contrast, George VI's list of possibilities reveals an almost ascetic and monk-like self-denial and absence of flesh-pots and high living. I dare say that some additional items have dropped away with the years but what is left is bleak in the extreme. There was, it is true, an occasional glass of Ayala's champagne, and we see that sometimes he clearly went a bust and ordered a steam tractor from Foden's or a Permutit Water Treating Equipment but otherwise it is a sober and hearteningly healthy and abstemious picture, with piping-hot Bovril straight from its HQ (yes, Bovril House, Enfield), Ryvita, Horlick's, bubbling soda-water from the Sodastream machine and, virtually the only outside excitement, a periodical visit from Trumper the Hairdresser. No chocs, No baps. No hams, and a fine example to the nearest and dearest.

Bang Bang You're Dead

I have only once, I am glad to say, let off a fire-arm in anger. This outburst of temper was long ago during military training on the outdoor rifle range at school, a spacious expanse of land made hideous by butts and set in a charming piece of country belonging to the Rothschild family, who kindly allowed us its use. We were part of the OTC or Officers Training Corps. Things may be different now but the school authorities of those days deceived nobody when they blandly announced that the action of joining the OTC was 'entirely voluntary'. In actual fact, it was about as voluntary as being born. At the age of 14, in you went: or else. Boys who were able to persuade their parents to invent excuses to get them off the detested eight-day summer camp found themselves next term moved down several places in seniority on the house list, a devastating punishment. They didn't opt out a second time.

Marched forth in column of fours to the range, we lay down in turns, were issued with live ammunition, adjusted our sights and prepared to shoot, while schoolmaster officers, as convincing in uniform as a No 3 touring company of *Journey's End*, barked out safety precautions before, during and after the pop-pop-popping. Could the cumbersome rifles have been Lee-Enfields? They certainly had the look of having served with Kitchener in his salad days. The anger of which I wrote came from the general idiocy of the undertaking, the appalling din, the bruising of one's shoulder, the humiliation of never hitting the target, the assorted smells, the heat, the scratchy uniforms, the buzzing flies and the realisation that nearby lay the cool, green, restful gloom of the Rothschild woods. How infinitely more profitable to lie there beneath a tree and read a good book, any book. But no.

Years passed and it was some time before I was called upon to let off a fire-arm again and on this occasion it was not in anger at all but more in a sort of hypnotised surprise than anything else.

The little happening occurred in France and during the somewhat confused fighting of 1940. I was in charge of an FSP section. FSP stood for Field Security Police, the word 'Police' being subsequently dropped as being needlessly off-putting, our mission being help and advice on the denying of information to the enemy. We consisted of 14 NCOs mounted on motor-bicycles, a sergeant-major, a car, and me. By May, 1940, I cannot think that there was much information that had been denied to the Germans: it was not very difficult to learn All from the leaky Frogs. Caught up in the extremely mobile military operations following the invasion of the Low Countries, we drove here, we drove there, occasionally shelled by tanks unable to find more interesting quarry, searching hastily deserted headquarters for documents valuable to the foe and knee-deep the entire time in suspected civilian spies brought to us for interrogation. Lacking concrete evidence, the British, strong on justice, usually liberated them. The French method of dealing with the problem was to question them and shoot them. The Belgian method was the same as the French, only without the questions.

One of the major difficulties was locating our various formations. You never knew where anybody had got to and when information reached you as to where they were, they weren't there any more. An officer friend of mine, coming in his car at dusk out of a side road, found himself in the middle of a German supply convoy ('*Guten Abend*') but managed, undetected, to slip away in the dark. Completely lost one day in Belgium, I mounted a hillock with my sergeant-major and, from its top, swept the counryside with the opera glasses entrusted to me by my father and previously mainly used for feasting the eyes on Gladys Cooper. They hung round my neck on a strap and made me look, I hoped, every inch the seasoned campaigner. Aircraft and guns and bangs and puffs of smoke were on all sides. Who was where, and which was which? Impossible to tell. Hearing from behind me a strange swooshing sound, I turned round and there, gliding relatively silently towards us and in highly deceitful manner, was a German aeroplane, about 300 feet up and quite near. Very unusual and interesting it was, but what to do for the best? I possessed a loaded revolver and, pulling it out, I drew a hasty bead and then pumped, as they say, a series of defiant shots into the very heart of the gleaming fuselage. Odd. It kept right on coming. My practice on that range had all been for nothing. It then dropped two mini-bombs which shook the ground, covered us in earth and killed a cow, after which it made itself scarce, startled by my revolver shots no doubt and realising that one meant business.

The pleasures of shooting, either in war or in peace, pass me by, though I am by no means averse, when it comes to birds, to the tasty results of the slaughter. And, a few decades ago, what wholesale slaughter it was, as the information published by Debrett's Peerage Ltd in *The Big Shots* (£6.50) and supplied by Jonathan Garnier Ruffer, shows. George V shot with Lord Burnham in 1913 when the day's bag was 4,000 pheasants. Lord Walsingham, shooting by himself on Blubberhouse Moor in 1888, bagged 1,070 grouse in a day (driven back and forth by beaters since dawn and worn out, some of them just sat sullenly down and sulked). Lord Ripon once dispatched 28 pheasants in a minute, seven of them being dead in the air at the same time, like jugglers with those Indian clubs. The record for the most individual kind of shot goes without question to the Duke of Devonshire who, aiming at a wounded cock pheasant as it passed a gate, managed, in one great glorious bang, to kill both the pheasant and the retriever that was running after it, while at the same time peppering the dog's owner in the leg, together with the Chatsworth chef who had unwisely come out to see the fun. Great consternation. Would dinner be on time?

Shooting was an ideal way for great landlords to entertain in the winter months. Edward VII ('Tum-Tum' behind his back), too obese for hunting, could safely be popped by his host into a butt and left there to blaze happily away at pheasants that had sometimes, like himself, arrived by train. The royal rip dearly loved banging off at almost anything that moved and on a Near East tour had ended the lives of wild boars, crocodiles and several owls. In Egypt he blasted dozens of flamingoes out of the morning flight, before going on to pick off a few bats in the tomb of Rameses IV. And he managed to bag a beater at Six Mile Bottom, the wounded man astutely realising that the louder he yelled, the larger the annuity was likely to be.

In fact, dangers were everywhere and not even the butts themselves were entirely safe. Lord Walsingham's powder exploded and he burst into flames, singeing his eyebrows. Lord Wemyss set fire, rather cleverly, to the butt itself, and thence to the surrounding countryside, which blazed pleasingly for a fortnight.

The book's photographs of the titled rich enjoying themselves, guns and death all round, hardly lift the heart though there are two surprises – Giacomo ('Tiny frozen hand') Puccini in a rather elaborate sable coat and bagging ducks, and the Archduke Franz Ferdinand, ready for the fray and who, in due course, got bagged himself.

Meals on Wheels

The thrilling news, flashed to an enthralled public by 'a popular daily', that Lady Falkender had braved the pickets and their placards (No More Upstairs Downstairs) outside Claridge's and had munched her lunch there, managing to conquer what must be her strong political distaste for such privileged places (she had soup and grilled steak, it seems, though salmon, Irish stew and steak-and-kidney pie were all fully obtainable and in the teeth, so to speak, of striking members of the kitchen staff), leads one on to muse on the subject of what, in the far from probable event of an ennoblement arriving for me at 'Myrtlebank', one would choose by way of a title. My fellow residents at Appleton would naturally expect and enjoy something resounding and showy, and why not indeed? It is true that 'Falkender' is a goodish bit more interesting than 'Williams' but baronesses in general don't really do all that well nowadays when offered a free choice of change of name. Dullness has not by any means been always the rule. Ponder for a moment on the melodious syllables of Baroness Gaby von Bagge of Boo, a challenge if ever there was one and a name whose authenticity is fully vouched for in that handy little volume of which I wrote an appreciation and which has happily resulted in correspondents kindly sending in a further supply of delightfully unusual names.

I am by nature both trusting and gullible but even I am not confident about the nominal bona fides of a gentleman from Co. Wicklow who signs himself (and types out the name too, for both legibility and good measure) Odious M. Spongebubble, apart from the simple fact that it is quite sufficiently unlikely to be true. However, from another and a wholly reliable quarter comes Norah J. Slapcabbage, and a crumpled newspaper cutting to prove it. A South African letter speaks of a Cape Town firm of undertakers cheerily named Human and Pitt, and I am verbally informed that there used to be similar funeral operatives in the Golders Green area called, and such a relief for all concerned,

Hurry and Bussell. Initials always give a name a flourish, with I.C. Shivers (incredibly by profession an iceman) and I.P. Frilli of Florence (hobbies unknown). There is a restaurant employee in New York called T. Hee and, living in the same fertile city, Horacine Clutch. And pity the sad fate of a Mrs Friendly Ley of California, whose chummy career came to a brisk end when her husband's revolver which he was cleaning, as any of us would, in the kitchen, went off by mistake.

In addition to the absorbing details of Lady Falkender's luxurious snackette, the popular daily concerned has also been splendidly informative and in the know about British Rail's exciting future plans for providing nourishment awheel. Whatever could they be, one thought, starting to read and with one's memories darting back to the long ago when it was, unbelievably, possible to ask the top-hatted station-master to be so good as to 'telephone ahead' and get them to put on a luncheon basket at Crewe or Darlington. And there, expectantly held aloft on the platform by a smiling (oh yes, they used to) buffet attendant, was a hamper of food with a bottle of chilled hock and a cold roast chicken beaming a welcome from among the lettuce and tomatoes. Nor was this just rich man's stuff, half a crown a head being the modest outlay.

And nearer today, I remember travelling by steam train to sunny Bournemouth, entranced at the discovery on the lunch menu of tasteful verbal adornments – 'dawn-fresh melon' it said (a friend swears to have seen 'dawn-gathered grapefruit'), followed by 'chef-carved beef' and 'minted peas' and 'oven-baked rolls' and we finally wound up, I can only suppose, with 'electrically-heated coffee'. Of what then could these BR novelties consist, I asked myself, feverishly reading on? Nothing very much, I'm afraid – 3p off biscuits and 4p off pork pies and 'our most expensive sandwich is only 35p'. I know that one mustn't live in the past but 35p is what used to be seven shillings and so what, pray, is that word 'only' doing?

However, if a laudable cheapness and economy is what they are truly after and aid to the impoverished denied both buffet and restaurant car (the latter currently gilded haunts solely of expense accounts), let me recommend to them an invaluable little booklet dated 1852, now reprinted by Scolar Press at the admirably economical price of 75p and entitled *A Plain Cookery Book for the Working Classes*, the gifted suggestions of none other than Queen Victoria's *maître d'hôtel*, Signor Elmé Francatelli. A thoughtful Introduction sets the tone by urging readers to rush out and procure a potato steamer and 'a mash-tub' and, with references to 'slender means', comforts one and all with the information that peasants all over Europe don't get very much to eat either. And then away we go with the main body of the work, inexpensive

British Rail's exciting future plans for nourishment awheel

recipes that set one salivating on sight and which I do hope British Rail will adopt for the future.

Picture us then all teed up in the restaurant car on the 12.30 from Paddington to Plymouth and, just as we're thundering through West Ealing, a waiter brings us the first delight, a stimulating *apéritif* in the shape of a glass of Toast Water (pour boiling water onto toast, it says, and leave till cool: 'it will then be fit to drink'). After this treat, and with satisfied hiccoughs ringing through the carriage and showers of 'Pardon' to accompany them, we tackle a bowl of sheep's head broth (split head into halves and toss in turnips), after which and with history-soaked Reading just visible through the steamy windows, it's a choice of stewed trotters, fried bullock's heart or baked cod's head, the cod featured in the illustration wearing an outstandingly grumpy and uncooperative expression – a member of some fish union, I dare say. With the sweet course, taken while flying through Pewsey at 90 m.p.h., I have to confess to a disappointment. Prominently listed, I find Brown and Polson Pudding, which I naturally took to be a pudding constructed from the tastier portions – buttocks, thighs, cheeks, – of Messrs Brown and Polson themselves, nestling in a suet crust and covered in their own custard but which turns out to be, rather tamely, a sort of lemon and arrow-root affair of very modest calorie content.

Kind Mr Francatelli does not, I am glad to say, confine himself solely to recipes and then just leave us in the lurch. Aware of the rich and indigestible nature of some of his dishes, he provides handy home remedies for various of the body's discomfitures and I am going to suggest to British Rail that, next to the restaurant car, they should hitch on a special Recovery Coach. Here, stretched out on divans as the train chugs into Westbury, we could sip peppermint cordials (wind), rice water (dysentery), treacle posset (colds), hyssop tea (worms), white wine whey (coughs), rice gruel (loose bowels) and an antispasmodic infusion laced with brandy (spasms). There is even a cure for chilblains. By Exeter, we'll all be as right as rain again.

So Nice to be Merry

For reasons that are truly incomprehensible to an aged journalistic nobody, I have in the past few years been interviewed on ten occasions. I can only assume that the kind and polite people concerned had 'done' everybody of interest and import- ance and were now down to the riff-raff at the bottom of the barrel. Faced with printing space or wave-bands to fill, they had become desperate. Five of the interviews were on telly, one on radio and four on paper and on behalf of journals. During all of them I tried not to look as totally astonished as I felt. I answered various questions and, when the venue was 'Myrtlebank', dis- pensed sherry and posed for snaps. I suspect that I was a bit of a disappointment as all but two of the interviewers, both of whom knew better, touched at some point on what they hopefully referred to as my 'serious side', trustfully imagining hidden depths of character and thought where no hidden depths exist.

And so I continue on my frivolous way and if I make so bold as to say that my first topic here is the late Queen Mary it is because she, among many virtues, knew on occasion how to abandon seriousness. When it wasn't too intellectually taxing, she enjoyed the theatre (she and George V went three times to *Rose Marie*) and was much taken, and how understandably, by a warm, witty and satirical revue staged post-war, and a stone's throw from the Brompton Road, at the little Boltons Theatre, then under the skilful management of John Wyse. How she ever came to hear of this treat, who can say, but there she was (again on three occa- sions) thumping out the rhythm of the livelier tunes with her parasol. Prior to her first visit, a tactful message had come from her lady-in-waiting to say that none of the fairly saucy material need be changed, which enabled gifted Billy Milton to sing a number called 'I'm the only Fakir on the Pier' (it went on, if memory serves, with 'And I'm feeling decidedly queer'). As she left, she bowed happily to all and sundry and kept saying *'Wasn't it good!'* It was indeed.

'It's quite beautiful to see' – Queen Victoria

I next saw her on what was for her a duty occasion but one that was only very slightly less light-hearted – the evening of ballet that re-opened Covent Garden the year after the war. She was with the king, the queen and the princesses, a splendidly regal figure (no parasol or tumpty-tum this time) advantageously placed in the royal box at what was visually the best end, the one furthest from the stage. During the second interval I noticed that Queen Mary, evidently keen to discover who was occupying the box next to her, had eased herself and her bust forward and was clearly bent on peering round the pillar for a look at her neighbours. At the same moment, I saw, to my great delight, that a jewel-encrusted occupant (one must assume a Duchess) had herself decided to see how things were going in the royal box and had similarly eased herself gently into position. They chose, as I hoped, the very same moment for peering round the barrier and found themselves dramatically nose to nose and, in the modern phrase, eyeball to eyeball. I have seldom seen two such startled ladies. Both heads shot rapidly back and thereafter kept themselves to themselves.

A hundred years before this event, the royal box at Covent Garden was frequently filled. Hitherto, one has somehow associated Queen Victoria's theatre-going solely with solemn command performances at Windsor or Osborne, with the widow in deepest mourning and creating pools of gloom from the front row. Nothing could be further from the truth and it is a happy astonishment to discover, from George Rowell's very charming *Queen Victoria Goes to the Theatre* (Elek, £6.95), what a keen student of the drama she was, and keen also on almost any other entertainment that was going, the visits all being excitedly recorded in her Journal. She particularly enjoyed circuses and was delighted to discover that the Drury Lane pantomime of 1838 included a turn by Van Amburgh's lions. Despite 'an awful squint of the eyes', Van Amburgh grappled with the animals, threw them to the ground while they angrily roared, and then lay on them: 'It's quite beautiful to see and makes me wish I could do the same' was the wistful and mind-boggling royal comment. As was to be her way, she returned repeatedly (seven times in six weeks) to the lions. The Drury Lane management, no fools, retained Van Amburgh when the pantomime was over and he incongruously popped up again at the end of Rossini's *William Tell*, through which Her Majesty had impatiently sat in order to get once more at those lions ('worth *more* than *all* the rest'). The unbridled love of entertainment was to continue, with a bit of a hiccough on Albert's death, all her life. The grumpy, sulky and legendarily unamused lady vanishes, to be replaced by the great enjoyer and laugher that she undoubtedly was. 'We were all in fits of laughter' is a regular Journal entry. 'How you have made me laugh!' she said to Mrs Bancroft after a performance at Balmoral. 'It is so nice to be merry.'

Her theatrical and operatic tastes were entirely catholic. Anything was worth trying once. She went to *Henry V*, *Lucia di Lammermoor*, *Figaro* and *O'Flanagan and the Fairies*, whatever that may have been. Farce (*His Last Legs*) was perfectly acceptable. The frequency of her visits is quite staggering. By 1852 she had been to Her Majesty's Theatre, only one of many London theatres, over 350 times. She went to first nights, considerably adding to the backstage agitations. She took, reprehensibly in my view, to 'dropping in' for an act of this or a scene of that. Like Queen Mary, no theatre was too remote for her (the tiny Olympic in Wych Street was constantly honoured). She conceived a strange fancy for the versatile Frederick Robson who, as well as act, could also dance and sing ('His song, terminating with the refrain "Diddle doo, diddle dum" quite haunts us'). And from one play she garnered a useful little phrase which she passed on to her eldest daughter in a letter: 'Now goodbye, my dearest, and as Papa says (the policeman says it in *Still Waters Run Deep*), "Keep up your pecker", meaning "keep up your spirits".'

It will not be supposed that when she went to a theatre, she left her critical faculties outside, but by and large everything was lovely and when Jenny Lind first came over, Victoria and Albert attended every one of her performances. And how convenient it was for entertaining visitors. Napoleon III and his Empress, arriving for a State visit (the Waterloo Chamber at Windsor was hurriedly rechristened the Portrait Gallery), were soon whizzed off to *Fidelio* ('Just as we were ready to go, the Emperor upset his cup of coffee over his cocked hat, which caused great amusement').

With the death of Albert, when his widow so signally failed to keep her pecker up, Victoria's theatre-going was over. Instead, the theatre came frequently to her, wherever she might be and at whatever inconvenience to the players. And there had always been ceaseless family amateur theatricals, with the future Edward VII doing good work in a German version of *Red Riding Hood*. 'Bertie did his part of the Wolf particularly well,' wrote his proud mother of this very early example of type-casting.

Flat On My Face

All serious readers who are of riper years will have no difficulty in remembering the pulsating schoolgirl stories from the gifted pen of Miss Dorita Fairlie Bruce and so popular did they and she become that in 1937 she went, if you understand me, into an omnibus. This was then a sure sign of solid success, for omnibus editions were, as indications of achievement, on a par with the modern paper-back. Second only in excellence to Miss Angela Brazil, the *fons et origo* of the genre, Miss Bruce indefatigably produced, also in 1937, her *Dimsie Intervenes,* a story containing that splendidly conscientious headmistress ('My dear, I am never off duty except when I'm in bed – and not always then') and the Anti-Soppist League, anxious to restore its old vigour to the school (some rather wet Juniors have been caught buying bath-cubes and freesia soap) by trooping down to the gym 'to practise those last leg movements of Miss Mallory's'. A previous Bruce *chef d'oeuvre* had been *Prefects at Springdale* (headmistress: Miss Timmins) in which a rather dotty Scottish recluse called Miss Peters offers a prize (gnarled dwarf cedar tree in 'a pot of exquis-ite Eastern workmanship') to the most go-ahead girl in the school, this attractive trophy being won, as you'll recall, by Marion Banister and Isolt Kingsley who vied in being go-ahead and tied for the prize, the other girls being far too busy having tre-mendous crushes on Miss Stewart, the games mistress ('She's got that – that sort of glamour') to be at all go-ahead.

I mention these weighty matters because I am just off to Scot-land for a short holiday and Miss Peters, of the exquisite pot, throws off from time to time such things as 'Hoots toots', words which I take to be an expression of either incredulity or irritation (incredulity will do fine for Springdale) and I am very anxious to pick up whatever I can in the way of useful Scottish phrases and expletives so as not to seem too much of a fish out of water when once north of the border. There is another Peters expression of which I feel I should be wary. It is, quite simply, 'Tits, Lassies!'

She says it really quite a lot. 'Lassies' I can follow. It is the meaning of the other, hidden or plain, that bothers me.

However, it is in my nature to be cautious and therefore, on alighting from the overnight sleeper at the station at Inverness and emerging into the town, I shall start slowly with 'Do you ken whether yon bonnie taxi by yon bonnie Bank of Scotland is free the noo?' Once inside the taxi and bowling along, I may risk something a little more elaborate – 'Och, blethers' perhaps, or 'kindly don't drive me widdershins'. The driver may care to know who and what one is ('Me hame's far awa in Devon') and I am full of hope that the rye will be ripe, or whatever. 'Gin a body meet a body' I shall cry, pointing, though I have no intention of pressing on with the rest of the poem which involved kissing between two persons of the opposite sex who seem to have had a casual encounter among the tall rye stalks, an activity quite unsuitable to my age and bound to cause comment (ALLEGED JOURNALIST ON SERIOUS CHARGE).

It is, I am sure, sensible not to put everything, wordwise, in the shop window at once, and therefore, like a wise general, I am keeping some of my troops in reserve, ready to rush them in in case the first assault hasn't silenced and flattened the opposition. One of these phrases is 'gude willie waught' and it occurs in the encore verses (which God forbid) of Auld Lang Syne. It means, as far as I've been able to work it out, a treble gin taken in friendly circumstances, not a bad thing to have up, so to speak, one's sleeve.

'My heart's in the Highlands' sang Robert Burns, hankering for the heights, 'a-chasing the deer.' I do not know whether my kind Scottish hosts will expect me to go stalking but here again I am, like a good boy scout, Prepared and I have equipped myself with the very latest word on the subject. This is a remarkable new book, *Monarchs of the Glen*, a history of this fascinating pastime by Duff Hart-Davis (Jonathan Cape sells it, finely illustrated, at £7.95 a time) and a regular mine of information about all personalities and aspects of the chase, if such it can be called, when much of the time one is apparently flat on one's face with heather shoots sticking up one's nose.

To a tyro such as I am certain to be, it is immensely heartening to learn what an ass Prince Albert used to make of himself. Apart from his almost complete lack of skill, he irritated everybody by saying that the inhabitants of Dalkeith looked like Germans and that Perth was like Basle. Birnam Wood (stationary for once) looked to him partly like Thüringen and partly like Switzerland (even when in Wales, the mountains reminded him, but nobody else, of Ischia). He horrified one and all by unsportingly banging blithely off from the dining-room window at some semi-tame deer in the park at Blair. Once, driving home with the Queen in a horse-carriage after a day on the hill, he sighted a stag, leant across his adoring wife and discharged his gun, practically under her nose but accurately for once, through the window. Does the intrepid monarch make mention in her diary of what must have been the deafening din, the smoke, the shock and the bolting horses? Not a bit of it. 'It was a very fine stag with nine points, quite dead. What luck!' For the rest of the time, Albert, keen as mustard, just rushed round missing everything ('Albert has been running about a good deal', the relentless diary notes) and dressed, if Landseer is to be believed, in a high and stiff white collar, light grey and tight-waisted frock coat, close-fitting check trousers, and kitted out with spats, deerstalker, white walking stick and gloves. Thus fully togged up his wonders to perform, he fired five shots into a pack of 200 deer without even the laws of mathematical probability coming to his aid. At times he just seems to have blazed away at anything that moved. Meantime his besotted better half scampered about after him, sometimes coming a purler in the heather ('I hurt my knee').

The Balmoral-based Victoria and Albert, together with Landseer's lifelike paintings, succeeded between them in making both deer-stalking and the Highlands extremely desirable socially. Persons of note flocked north at appropriate times and picked off their prey. Reproductions of 'The Stag at Bay' and 'The Deer Drive' brought the somewhat bloody excitements of the sport into almost every home in the land. The government of the day, deciding on what was the right and tasteful thing to do, commissioned 'The Monarch of the Glen' from Landseer to fill an empty panel in the House of Lords Refreshment Room, but briskly withdrew ('Sorry. Venison's off'), and with the paint scarcely dry, the money suggested. The painting went instead to Lord Londesborough, who subsequently sold it at a profit that can only be called thumping. Not, alas, the last time that a government made financial fools of themselves.

Come Along Up

We tend to wake early in Appleton for our bedtime the night before is seldom unduly delayed and the soft Devon air generally induces cavernous yawns just after dear Angela Rippon has depressed one and all with her news and has smiled her last. Joyous birdsong renders alarm-clocks quite unnecessary and shortly after 6.30 a.m. the stately peace of 'Myrtlebank' is broken by the tinkle of a tea-cup. Those who like to imagine, in their friendly way, that I have at command relays of uniformed domestics only too glad to rise at first light, dust, scour, polish and activate the Aga, must think again. I make the tinkling sound myself, likewise the cheering tea that fills the welcome cup. Though sugar is said to be disastrous for old fatties, I pop in a generously heaped spoonful or two. What the hell.

I descend to the kitchen to do all this and shall continue to do so, having been totally baffled on a recent visit to North Wales ('Any Questions?' from ozone-packed Colwyn Bay) by finding in my hotel bedroom one of those mechanical tea-making appliances that switch on lights, trigger off buzzers and brew tea but which unfortunately demand a degree of co-operation from the user. I read the admirably detailed instructions four times, gazed in despair at the adjustable controls and dials and became increasingly bemused. It first told one what to do, all of them actions well beyond my scope, and when it came to the list of warnings about what *not* to do, the Ten Commandments weren't in it. This, I saw at once, was not for me. I did however manage to extract the actual tea-pot from the main body of the machine and, feeling guilty, fill it from the bathroom tap's near-boiling water and, with the aid of a dainty tea-bag, construct a more or less acceptable cup.

Next day, departure from this bracing and popular resort coughed up one of those perplexities with which modern life bristles. Three of us had to return by train to London, and railway enthusiasts (if that can still be the word) will wish to know details

44

Something large and chunky and attractive in lederhosen

of our trip. It was roughly a four hour ride and a corkingly hot day but there were no buffet car or liquid availabilities of any sort. I assume that there was a guard on the train, though I did not see him. Perhaps he preferred to remain, so fast did we fly, near the emergency brakes. If there was a ticket-collector, he too chose to be invisible. Possibly he had had distressful news from home and was quietly crying in the luggage-van. At Euston nobody took our tickets or showed the slightest interest. We could have done the whole journey for nothing. A weird way, as has been said, to run a railroad.

Back now to Glorious Devon and there every morning I am, by 6.45 a.m. or so, tucked up again in bed, laden tray to hand and with the first healing draught of Typhoo gurgling its way down, all ready to face the BBC's Third Programme and often soothed by the mellifluous tones of Patricia Hughes, who could announce the very direst tidings without causing the faintest alarm ('The end of the world is expected in an hour's time, and meanwhile, and as requested by Mrs Henderson of Station Crescent, Bath, here is Debussy's *'L'après-midi d'un faune'* '). Radio 4 is, at that time too, apt to be full of pearls. On occasion, religious matters are toward and a cleric dispenses professional bromides to explain away the world's horrors. The other day we were informed, as though it were a stunningly fresh tit-bit of news, that God doesn't always answer prayers at once. Like 7p letters, delays are to be expected. The general theme, a throaty voice advised, should be 'Give God Time', a phrase which I chose to interpret penally and instantly gave Him twenty years' hard labour for all the dreadful misery and bother He puts us to.

With prayers go, of course, cosy reassurances of an after-life. A recent pronouncement on this doubtful possibility came from an old friend of mine, a charming hostess much given to entertaining and who, looking anxiously round her drawing-room, said despairingly 'But there are so *many* of us. I really don't see how God is going to get us all *in*.' Another view was expressed a few years ago by Sir John Gielgud: 'I'm sure there isn't an after-life. If there were, Ivor Novello would have got a message to us.' If Sir John is wrong, how delightful to picture the telegram arriving and being pinned up in some theatrically central place, perhaps the Globe Theatre foyer in Shaftesbury Avenue. EVERYTHING HERE TOO DIVINE FOR WORDS STOP GOD A COMPLETE AND UTTER DARLING STOP COME ALONG UP STOP LOVE IVOR.

When Mary Martin in *South Pacific* sang that she was going 'to

46

wash that man right out of my hair', she was, as far as theatre history is concerned, washing a good many other men too, Ivor among them. The day of his type of musical, and what a melodious and splendid day it had been, was coming to an end. Tuneful twaddle was on the way out. Leading ladies were no longer to 'enter singing' as Mary Ellis had so triumphantly done as a Viennese operatic star in *The Dancing Years*, sweeping, warbling away, up that hill to the country inn from which Ivor had just, and his grand piano conveniently with him, been kicked out by his rentless and relentless landlady.

When the Novello musicals were at Drury Lane, spectacle, in the great tradition of that immense theatre, was the thing. If a train puffed on, it was bound to have a noisy accident in those clouds of escaping steam that conceal the cardboard. No huge liner appeared that did not later sink rather slowly to allow the audience to drink in the harrowing scene and to wonder if Ivor had been rescued. Yes, yes. He had. In *Careless Rapture* we were momentarily in China and it needed no seismograph to tell us why. When the distant rumbling started, the heroine, Dorothy Dickson, found herself on one of those somewhat frail Chinese balconies and required to speak one of the stage's most remarkable lines: 'My maid says it's earthquake weather'. How right she was. It was said that at the dress rehearsal, the hinged scenery stubbornly refused to collapse and extras had to go rushing on, nobly ad-libbing ('Oh what a terrible earthquake!') and push huge buildings to the ground.

Rodgers and Hammerstein, coupled with the names of *Oklahoma, Carousel, South Pacific* and *The King and I*, put an end to such luscious make-believe, though perhaps they did slip back a bit with *The Sound of Music*, much of which was altogether too good to be true. When the number 'My Favourite Things' occurred, I had a private fantasy about one of the elderly nuns. The 'favourite things' were, as you'll recall, snowflakes on kittens and white woollen mittens and such like, but not for my nun. *Her* favourite things were altogether more basic – platefuls of sausages and sauerkraut, stein after stein of lager, and something large and chunky and attractive in lederhosen.

Nothing Like a Dame

The alleged loneliness of the long distance runner is as nothing compared with that of the stand-up comedian who, much as he might wish to, cannot run but must stay right there where he is, centre-stage and alone and make us laugh. Of all theatrical assignments, and I include King Lear, this is by far the toughest. The first such entertainer that I ever saw, about 60 years ago, was in a pantomime and in the person of a male Mrs Crusoe, the mother of Robinson, a sprightly widow scraping a living as proprietress of a seaside boarding-house. With her orange hair permanently in curlers, she had a wealth of red flannel petticoats and scarlet bloomers constantly on view as she tripped repeatedly up ('Drat them bollards!') upon the quayside, her elastic-sided boots in all directions. In due course she was to be found, alone, upon six foot of stage in front of a flapping drop-curtain ('A street in Porttown'). Here, while invisible behind her the quayside was noisily changed to the deck of the Saucy Sue, the harassed hotelier told us of her late husband's marital infidelities ('My last child didn't resemble him at all') and her current worries, both culinary ('They won't touch my dumplings') and financial ('I have no money but my aunt has piles').

As a seasoned, not to say hardened, theatre-goer, I never imagined that the evening would come when I would gladly pay £3 to Barry Humphries for a stall seat in which to be cheerfully abused, handed a gladiolus (a real one, surprisingly) and instructed when to stand up and wave it to and fro (mine bent in the middle and hung down, producing a storm of criticism and doubt about my abilities in other directions). Prior to this activity, Mr Humphries had managed to persuade a nice married lady called June to give us the fullest imaginable details of her bathroom – colour of tiles round the bath ('a sort of fawn'), floor covering (lino in a 'fancy pattern'), curtains (swallows a-wing), the exact siting of the lavatory pan, the assortment of 'toilet requisites', and so on.

At each new horrific detail, Dame Edna Everage, for it was she, beamed her appreciation and gave a glad cry of 'Why June, that sounds just exquisite!' Near June was seated a dusky foreigner whom Dame Edna chose to consider as being deaf, illiterate and dotty and to whom, through his shouts of delighted and hysterical laughter, she explained, elaborately mouthing, what was going on. In addition to his stage appearances, Mr Humphries has been widely exposed to the public on the telly, graciously receiving Miss Joan Bakewell in his 'simulated kitchen-dinette' and handing her some splendidly obscene-looking items of food. I do realise that you either like him or you don't and I make no apology for rating him, purely as a laughter-provider, as highly as I have (now in the past, alas) rated Miss Beatrice Lillie. Their techniques and material are poles apart, with the elegant Miss Lillie so restrained and coolly professional, and Dame Edna a great galumphing, hoydenish, warm-hearted amateur (as he lets it appear) but the results are the same.

Voracious, as they say, readers who can devour almost anything will have been prepared for Mr Humphries and for the breezy impact of Australia in general by the production by Messrs Collins a few years ago of *My Day*, selections from the diary of the wife of the then Prime Minister, Mrs Gough Whitlam, a lanky charmer from down under. There one read, fascinated, of her bedroom suite and the beige butterfly wallpaper, her blinds printed with 'coloured vegetables', weekends in the restful peace of Bondi Junction, the occasional comb-up at Radford's hairdressing salon, the shopping at Tall Gals and the games of golf ('I went berserk around a bunker'). There were also the free use of the adjectives 'super' and 'beaut', the multi-vitamin pills swallowed before a breakfast of fried lamb's brains with tomato ketchup, the occasional challenges ('Hands up those who know where Eaglehawk is') and confessions ('I'm not a poetry person'), the evening dress 'decorated with light garlands of wattle blossom in sequins', and the sipping, on festive occasions, of Seppelts Great Western Chablis and Penfolds Minchinbury Champagne ('the queen of all beverages').

From this somewhat weird reality it is but a short step to Dame Edna's world. No holds at all are barred by Mr Humphries and here, to relish during his absence from us, is an offering 'for the fans who crave some literary token from my quill', *Dame Edna's Coffee Table Book*: Limp Edition (Harrap, £3.95), 'a guide to gracious living and the finer things of life' and starting with, in early days, a Passion Play appearance as Mary Magdalene (the local chemist couldn't manage frankincense and myrrh so they compromised with a jar of Valderma and some Sloane's liniment, Mary subsequently rinsing her hair with a squirt of Loxene in a deconsecrated font backstage). Secure against her family background of three 'gorgeous kiddies', a hubby, Norm, prostrate with prostate, and the finest collection of diamanté costume jewellery in the Southern Hemisphere, we find this indomitable 'honours graduate from the University of Life' now happily telling us how to pronounce useful cultural names (Mik-ell-anne jello. You-jean-Goose-ends), now musing on the ups and downs of a dentist's career ('How would you like to spend your time up-to-your-wrists in other people's dribble?').

There are sections on yoga, navel hygiene, crow's-feet ('What are crow's-feet but the dried up beds of old smiles?'), and the physical shortcomings of her old friend and bridesmaid, Madge Allsop ('I felt it my duty to put my foot down firmly on her facial hairs'). Most important of all is My Nightly Countdown to Natural Beauty and what to do, while sleeping, to help 'skin and crevice care' – place two soothing cuke discs on the eyes (secure them with Sellotape), pamper your brow with nourishing nana strips (sticky-side down), clamp a couple of juicy lemons on your armadillo elbows, feed your hungry face tissues ('a mayonnaise mask is perfect'), and try at all costs to sleep on your back.

When it comes to some of Dame Edna's recipes, one hardly knows what to believe, so persuasive do they sound. I think we can rule out Braised Emu Leg, Possum Pumpkin Pie ('a barbecue bonanza') and Bandicoot Stewed in Milk, despite the telling addition of '1 small blade of mace'. But what of a fish dish called Groper Surprise ('the most luscious parts are the immense gelatinous lips'), or Curried Rabbit in Grapefruit Cases, Moomba Meat Balls and Ravioli and Date Layer? Wiser not to attempt them, I suppose, but the whole fun lies in the fact that Dame Edna's activities, attitudes, clothes and bracing outlook are so close to the real thing that you cannot with confidence tell one from the other.

Thoroughly Modern Mimi

The original production, by Sir Barry Jackson at the Kingsway Theatre in 1925, of *Hamlet* in modern dress caused quite a little stir by its novelty and found every dramatic critic for once in benevolent mood ('How freshly the great old play comes up', etc). The years have somewhat blurred one's memory of the details of dress and scenery but the gloomy Dane himself seemed to be almost permanently in roomy plusfours and brogues, like the then Prince of Wales, and just in from a refreshing round of golf with Horatio on the testing Elsinore links, Francisco probably picking up a little pin-money as caddy. As to the Queen, the sartorial example of the wife of the living monarch of the time, Queen Mary, would have been of negligible value as a trendsetter and, for day wear, Gertrude would almost certainly have plumped for a flecked tweed two-piece in bottle green with dyed musquash collar. Polonius was, of course, top-hatted and in a tail coat, with poor old Osric looking perfectly idiotic in mauve Oxford bags.

Dressing players and setting plays in periods and places not their own has become a commonplace and we now think little of the practice, merely keeping a watchful eye out for any happy inventions that the director may have dreamt up (Lady Macbeth feverishly polishing her bifocals to help her read the letter which, written by her ambitious husband in a state of considerable excitement and exaltation, may well have been legible only with difficulty). The other night, watching on the telly a pleasing performance of *Hänsel und Gretel*, I fell to wondering why the directors of operas have gone in so little for up-dating and playing about with the musical works entrusted to their care. In a present-day *La Bohème*, for instance, Mimi and those artists would be 'squatting', protected from the law and with no rent payable, in their respective attics, surrounded by colour TV sets obtained from social security benefits, with Mimi's cold little hands snug and warm in Kozystretch wool-substitute mittens

The gloomy Dane almost permanently in roomy plus fours and brogues

provided by the local branch of the W.I. And as she swallows her health-service cough-linctus, she looks forward to the day when she is old enough for Age Concern to bring her meals on wheels.

It is true that in the *Hänsel und Gretel* of which I write, the wicked witch was to be seen spying out her gingerbread prey through a pair of periscope army fieldglasses and looking momentarily like the opponent that Field-Marshal Montgomery always referred to as Wommel, but with the first scene of all, what an opportunity was missed. The children, you'll recall, are alone in their parents' cottage, Hänsel making brooms and Gretel knitting stockings. Day is waning, they are both hungry, and a kindly neighbour, knowing the family's poverty, has brought them something for supper. And guess what it is? A jug of milk, if you please. At the sight of it, Hänsel becomes thoroughly over-excited, but what modern child would dream of accepting just plain milk for supper? There was a chance here for the good neighbour to struggle in with fish fingers and chips, bottles of Pepsi-Cola and cartons of raspberry yoghurt. Then when the mother returns, instead of accidentally knocking over the dull old milk, she can send the fish fingers flying and slop the yogurt down her dress. Much more realistic and in keeping with the times. The children would, when caught and baked in the oven, become either Mars Bars or Crunchies.

An opera that could benefit enormously from up-to-the-minute treatment is *Tristan und Isolde*. The Irish Princess Isolde, coming over by ship to wed King Mark of Cornwall, a province which has, as you see, set a fine example of extreme devolution, is normally discovered, attended by her handmaiden, Brangäne (a muddler, obtained from who knows which domestic agency), in a sort of scruffy tent on deck, the purpose of the canvas shield being to stop the crew entertaining impure thoughts at the sight of females afloat. The last time I travelled from America to England it was on the Q.E.II and we put in for a time to Cork harbour. Here it would be a simple matter for Isolde to board the liner and thus our very first glimpse of her would be in her slap-up stateroom on A Deck, through whose inner portholes Tristan could feast his eyes on her blond plaits. In addition to her loud, tuneful voice, we know that Isolde has abilities as a dispensing chemist (love potions and poisonous draughts a speciality) and a sizeable medicine-chest and some parcels from Boots catch the eye on a table between the twin beds (she's doubling up with poor old Brangäne, a martyr to sea-sickness and forever stuffing herself with Kwells). Diplomas on the cabin walls from the scientific departments of Dublin and Belfast universities, together with certificates from the St John's Ambulance, bring us right into the 20th century and complete the picture of a studious, gifted girl about to cut short a promising career in the field of healing and make a most unfortunate marriage.

The whole of Wagner, indeed, lies before us, simply crying out for modern treatment. The laced bodice and floating peach-coloured draperies, albeit with tin helmet and armoured stomacher, into which Brünnhilde is usually thrust are laughably inadequate for the arduous, rocky, assaultcourse work that is expected of her. Her dainty footwear is particularly unsuitable. Nobody can ride a horse, lug dead heroes about and be ready for the boudoir all in one breath, so to speak. The proper attire for Brünnhilde is Tyrolean mountaineering rig – stout boots, alpenstock, coils of rope, lederhosen and a hat with a saucy feather in it. A rucksack festooned with camping equipment would show her to be a girl who really means business. She can change into something more filmy and appealing later on, though Siegfried will easily spot the woman beneath the envelope, even when she is suitably kitted out for the heights. Siegfried himself must, of course, discard those rather mangy fur garments that carry us back to the dear old days of the invaluable Clarksons of Wardour Street and show himself for the man he is in cerise, male model, Y-fronted posing briefs. That sword, about which such a tremendous fuss is made, should be clearly marked as having been manufactured by Messrs Wilkinson.

When Siegfried finds the sleeping Brünnhilde on the tippy-topmost rock and kisses her awake, they plight their troth and betrothal gifts are exchanged. Here, alas, we can do very little as the presents themselves (he to her, a ring: she to him, an extremely large horse) are important plotwise, but an inventive director could add on a few little extra tokens of appreciation of the kind often found on any wedding gift list – a phosphor-bronze coal-scuttle, a nest of walnut occasionals, matching disposal-bins, a croquet set, kebab skewers. Then the lovers, doubtless exhausted by the day's excitements and naturally wishful to put their feet up and rest awhile, go off into, of all uncomfortable quarters for such a moment, a rough cave. This won't do at all. I suppose it's a bit too much to expect a luxi-motel at that altitude, and their absence of luggage might cause raised eyebrows at the desk, but at the very least Brünnhilde could rummage about in her equipment, drag out her inflatable Up-In-A-Jiffy collapsible tent and rubber mattress and get busy blowing. She's got, heaven knows, the lungs for it.

Always Wave to Trains

There are, when you come to think of it, very few people in life whom you kiss lovingly on the forehead. Enterprising wanderers down love's by-ways may well stumble upon more exotic areas to salute (is it the Burmese who take such a lively interest in the backs of friends' knees?) but the forehead is a sort of chaste and hallowed zone reserved for true love and respectability and it was here that, in my youth, my mother would kiss me on those days when she was especially pleased with me. The occasions were, understandably, rather rare. I was an ill-behaved and deeply unattractive child, dreaded in every nursery in SW13 and from a very early age I bore a close facial resemblance to my paternal grandmother who, in her turn, was the living image of Queen Victoria when widowed and in huffy mood. Family snaps reveal me either frowning displeasingly or scowling or pouting or rage-fully blubbing, a repellent spectacle, dreadfully obese and with several double-chins which in second childhood have returned richly to me, bringing a few friends with them.

We were a firmly middle of the middle-class family and in those days such families always had nannies for their children. My nanny was kind enough not to consider me nearly as poison-ous and uncuddlesome as I now clearly realise I was. She was calm and patient and unfailingly obliging. I used to find railways, either model or real, totally fascinating and she allowed me, with my arms and hands stretched out before me, to pretend to be a railway engine and, loudly puffing, to run full tilt into the cosy and shock-absorbing 'buffers' on her chest. Invited on Sunday to join my parents for dessert after lunch, a frequent treat, I made mention of our railway game and of nanny's buffers, greatly confusing my father, never the quickest chap to absorb a new concept, who plainly had visions of a series of old gentlemen whom nanny had managed to enslave. As I grew older, our afternoon walks on Barnes Common often led us to the railway line that runs, I think, east to Clapham Junction and Waterloo and westwards to Mortlake and Richmond and goodness knows what further excitements beyond. There we would stand and wait for a train to pass. Nanny's view was that everybody, and children particularly, should always wave to trains ('You never know, somebody nice might see you and wave back'). This was better, outward-looking advice for a child than she perhaps realised and I have been wildly waving, in a different sense, ever since. There have been, I must confess, one or two somewhat bizarre responses but on the whole the readiness to wave and risk a snub has brought, in terms of friendship and interest, an enormous gain. Better than at Barnes, indeed, where the trains seemed to be only electric ones and were, in the afternoons, relatively empty. Not good waving material. Wavings back were few and far between but one or two a week just about kept us going and on the alert for more.

This early training has caused me to be all in favour of the reading of horoscopes by those lucky enough to take newspapers and magazines which feature them. Horoscopes too are outward-looking and encourage people to be expectant and on the *qui vive* for novelties, either human or material. It helps the day along to wonder about that 'letter from abroad', the new friendship to be made at work (Mr Bagshaw, from head office, graciously unbending and suggesting lunch at Spotti's and to hell with your vouchers), the elderly relative who is going to 'turn up trumps' (presumably by turning up his toes and leaving you everything). Optimism is the general tone and only very occasionally do they strike a discouraging note ('The afternoon is not a good time for gardening') or deal in relative gloom ('Somebody on whose judgment you rely will unexpectedly leave the country', *not* under a cloud, one does hope). Ladies' magazines are splendid providers of horoscopic material and some of them even go further and, studying your stars with immense concentration, add helpful tips ('Play up your eyes and your classic bone structure') for emphasising your sex appeal ('Aim for the still-waters-run-deep look').

I have recently been reading a number of horoscopes and in particular the sections devoted to my very own astral sphere (Taurus, of all the unsuitable animals) and, my word, 1977 is going to be an interesting year down in Devon! I discount, of course, the vague statements that crop up, such as 'On Tuesday, anything could happen'. Of course it could, unless I'm careful. Then there is 'a possibility of good news from afar'. How far is afar in the world of astral divination? Do they mean Mars or merely Newton Abbot? Imprecision gets us nowhere. And what can one make of 'later in the month your affairs will get a boost'? What affairs? Financial or *du coeur*? It's far too late for either to be any sort of real help. Certain prognostications, however, are quite clear and do indeed apply to my happy country existence. 'An older relation could surprise you' it says.

At my age I am a bit short of older relations so this can only be my Cousin Madge, now nudging 86. She may well surprise me but not, I do trust, by taking to her horse and trap again (her last trip to Exeter and back, some years ago, took her 11 hours and she was far from welcome in the Cathedral car park, the attendant insisting that the facility was only intended for horseless carriages. The horse was called Ajax and it had a morbid passion for geraniums). Then comes a brightness – 'A sociable evening will find friends in sparkling mood'. Hooray! This obviously means the Bultitudes, and in top form, splashing out on a dinner party to celebrate the latest Gallup Poll figures (Mrs Thatcher up a point or two), with the Colonel regaling us with sporting yarns from his lifelong battle against fur and feather, and Mrs Bultitude a vision in a multi-print silk sarong top-piece and flared harem trousers (Miss Entwhistle's disapproving sniffs can be heard in Exeter). But now, a riddle: 'A splendid day for buying home equipment', is hotly followed by 'Control your wanderlust'. There's a teaser, with instructions for action coupled with a plea for inaction. One wants so much to do the right thing. If I go to Torquay (nine miles) and buy a washing-machine, will that rate as wanderlust and will due retribution come later ('On Thursday, something unpleasant will stop you in your tracks' is planned for Aquarians but could well be diverted my way)? Better not to chance it.

The *TV Times*, chock-a-block with good things almost all connected with TV, has, surprisingly, its own horoscope section, 'Zodiac and You', together with further helpful information under the heading 'Stay Healthy With the Heavens'. Turning eagerly to my own health section, I find 'Taureans are the heavyweights of the zodiac. They put on extra flesh around the neck and thighs in particular.' No need to be insulting, and my thighs are my own affair, but perhaps there's something in this star business after all.

No Laughing Aloud

The father-son relationship, never an easy business at the best of times, is not helped when the elder of the two is a well-intentioned but boring gas-bag, given to sounding off in a somewhat self-righteous manner on the widest possible variety of subjects. I am referring, of course, to the 18th-century Earl of Chesterfield and it is true that in the relationship under review the son in question was at first a godson and the godfathers of those days doubtless took their spiritual duties very seriously. Later on the boy became an adopted and much loved son but it seems to me unforgivable to off-load such a daunting pile of verbiage onto somebody not your own flesh and blood and who therefore has done nothing, so to speak, to deserve it. One is further appalled to find that the son, Master Philip Stanhope, a child resident 'at Mr Roberts' boarding house in Marybone', was aged six when the torrent of advice and maxims first descended, in letter form, upon him.

From then on the missives poured in, outlining rules of conversation and droning away about scandal, parsons, diligence ('Idleness is only the refuge of weak minds'), knowledge, women (very poorly rated), with impertinent criticisms of Shakespeare thrown in. Even when Philip advanced in years and passed on to Dr Dodd's scholastic establishment near Twickenham, on flowed the pen of this poor man's La Rochefoucauld and who indeed sometimes wrote in French and included lists of handy words and phrases (*de mal en pis*: from bad to worse) to be mastered. There was no escape.

And the result of all this? One is delighted to report that, for all his lordship's high hopes of high office for him in the future, the boy, though kind and gentle, turned out to be nothing but an amiable and commonplace nonentity. Of heavy build, he enjoyed French cooking and was a careful keeper of weather records (he knew, heaven knows, all about wind), emptying the rain-gauge daily and noting down the precipitations in a large book. So much for good advice to the young. It is odd that one of Lord Chesterfield's statements still has the power, even after 200 years, to make one bristle with rage. 'In my mind there is nothing so ill-bred as audible laughter.'

What sort of discouraging twaddle was that to feed to a healthy boy of nine? At that age he should have been loudly splitting his sides every minute of the day. But possibly this was, and maybe still is, a widely held upper-crust view of laughter. Perhaps Lord Grade could smuggle a decibel counter into the House of Lords and watch the needle's wobbles, if any. I have certainly heard Lady Diana Cooper state that she had never in her life reacted physically to anything she found funny but I dare say that famous beauties have always found it wiser not to go in for any facial activities that in any way might stretch or disturb or unseat the peaches and cream. It may be too that Goldsmith's warning that loud laughs speak a vacant mind froze people's cackles in their throats, though this rubbishy view is disproved by many distinguished laughers, among them Maurice Bowra, a man with a mind

A man may not marry his grandmother

that could hardly be called vacant and whose reactions to anything, either grave or gay, prduced thunderous volumes of sound.

Be all this as it may, in childhood and youth I was encouraged, on all suitable occasions, to laugh, and I was lucky enough to find myself surrounded by contemporaries as keen on laughter as I was. We actively sought it out. A fellow schoolboy called Williamson, aged 12, became convinced that, if only one knew where to look, the Bible could provide rib-ticklers galore, the Old Testament particularly. Despite constant discouragements he pored through book after book for guffaws, and certainly unearthed, in Proverbs, a few things that were unusual. 'Dead flies cause the ointment of the apothecary to send forth a stinking savour.' Meant to be funny, we wondered? Who can now say? And what about 'As a jewel of gold in a swine's snout, so is a fair woman who is without discretion'? History is silent.

One Sunday, in the local church where the school attended divine service and during a missionary's sermon (it was, ahead of its time, concerned with 'being kind to Brother Fuzzy-Wuzzy'), I saw Williamson beginning to shake. He had been ferreting about in the Book of Common Prayer and, silently pointing, discreetly passed me his discovery. It was under the Table of Kindred and it said: 'A man may not marry his grandmother.' One of Williamson's grandmothers, a frequent visitor to the school, was a dear, grey-haired, roly-poly lady called Mrs Rumball. She used to arrive in a stately chauffeur-driven car and take us out to tea. The idea of Williamson being joined in unholy matrimony to Mrs Rumball ('I Humphrey, take thee, Clarice . . .') provided a delightful hilarity.

When in due course at school the frightful Latin lessons eased up and we could concentrate more on French and German, my heart leapt at the information that we were going to read some 'plays'. I knew what to expect from plays, having been taken by parents and jolly aunts during the hols to *Rookery Nook*, *Hay Fever* and *The Farmer's Wife*. Chuckles, one felt, were just around the corner. But nobody, alas, had warned me about the plays of Racine and Corneille. Racine and Corneille were very far from being funsters. If Racine and Corneille knew any jokes, they kept them to themselves. They really do not make suitable reading material for 15-year-olds who are ready for a lark. Their plays did, however, at least label themselves as being 'tragedies'.

I had not yet realised that anything that was not positively tragic proclaimed itself to be a 'comedy', however unfunny. If actually funny, it called itself 'a light comedy' (Alfred Lunt, asked by an interviewer why each play in which he and Miss Fontanne so brilliantly appeared was always described as 'a light comedy', answered crisply 'Well, would *you* buy tickets for something that called itself "A heavy comedy"? No sir, you would not.'). And so, when our German master (alas, no scintillater) announced 'a comedy' by Lessing called *Minna von Barnhelm*, I was all attention, with a pleased smile at the ready. Barnhelm gets 0 out of 10 for merriment and charm. Bad cess to, if it actually exists, Barnhelm. If you are an RAF pilot and happen to have a bomb handy, pray go at once and drop it on Barnhelm. Flatten Barnhelm. And if Minna chances to be in Barnhelm at the time, so much the better.

In Gratitude

How odd is the extraordinary variety of the persons who, not always for a very apparent reason, catch the public imagination and remain for ever of interest. Crippen, for example, a shoddy and inefficient little murderer. Mata Hari, both a bad dancer and a doubtful spy. Some achieve it mainly by an early death. I always maintain that if Lawrence of Arabia and Isadora Duncan were still living in querulous retirement as OAPs in a run-down private hotel in Bognor, nobody would give them a second thought. Sometimes inactivity does the trick. The reputation of E. M. Forster, who was already to some minds rather too highly rated, increased to giant proportions with every silent year that passed. The matchless Lunts, ever modest, have claimed that they only became really famous the moment they gave up acting and nobody could see them any more. It pains me to couple the name of W. Somerset Maugham with that of Crippen but he, too, is one of whom the public will never let go. Biographers will, till kingdom come, be having a go at him and digging here, ferreting there.

The latest offering by Frederic Raphael has just been published by Thames and Hudson at £3.95. The book's illustrations, strangely inept here and there, reveal the shape of facial things to come – the sad, serious orphan boy and the gloomy scholar of King's School, Canterbury. Mr Raphael's is a conscientious attempt at a fair biography but the text reveals little that was not already widely enough known and carries with it less than hearty appreciation of both Mr Maugham and his works. That face would be glummer still.

As I said, it pains me because he was a friend. I was lucky enough to stay with him and his companion, Gerald Haxton, at the Villa Mauresque at Cap Ferrat a number of times in the Thirties and, though Gerald was dead by then, also after the war. Beyond displaying extreme pleasure at his jokes, which were more frequent and funnier than some may imagine, I had little to offer either socially or intellectually and he must have found me a bore but he was far too polite and kind to show it. If I had things to say, I was, anyhow, in those days far too shy to say them. Willie, as I was soon allowed to call him, had great charm and beautiful manners but he could be chilling and one didn't risk a bromide in his presence. The villa was large and comfortable. The food was perfect. There were bathing and tennis and trips in the yacht. There was a wonderful garden and guests had a whale of a time. I

If Isadora Duncan were still living in querulous retirement in Bognor

suppose that in the climate of today I ought to be feeling ashamed of enjoying such privilege and hedonistic activities. Well I am not.

Some quirk in his character made him not greatly mind when people behaved badly. He expected them to, for he had no high opinion of human nature and when events supported his view he was not really displeased. Gerald Haxton could be relied on to provide him, periodically, with stimulating jolts. One day at the villa there was what was, for me, a lunch party of an impressive kind for among the guests were G. B. Stern, Elizabeth ('German Garden') Russell and H. G. Wells. Elizabeth Russell, living nearby in France, had written a book of enormous charm and humour, *The Enchanted April*, and it was fascinating to meet her. She was indeed enchanting. She told us that she never attempted to conform to summer time or French hours or ever to alter her clocks ('I'm very hungry. You see, it's half past three by my inside'). When Willie wasn't looking, Gerald, who had a problem, darted to the drinks table and briskly lowered half a tumbler of neat gin. We went into lunch, somewhat formally, and sat down. Willie, searching about for something with which to start conversational balls rolling, said genially 'I've just had a h-h-hot bath' (when writing of him, it is essential to indicate the stammer). Gerald, semi-tipsy, gave a snort of disgust at this banality, leant forward and said loudly and clearly, 'and did you masturbate?' A terrible silence fell as we scooped up our avocados. But Willie had been asked a question, and questions must be answered, if with difficulty. There were some anguished facial contortions and finger snappings, which sometimes helped, and then came 'As it h-h-h-happens, n-n-n-n-no.' We ate on.

At less formal and more relaxed meals, interesting matters emerged, among them the unusual behaviour of his brother Frederick, the Lord Chancellor. 'I've always sent him tickets for my first nights, and first editions of my b-b-b-books, but he's never even acknowledged one of them or let it be known, even by mistake, that he'd seen the play or read the book. Isn't he a sh-sh-sh-shameful fellow!' He knew well how sometimes to use the stammer to the best advantage. During the Thirties, many of the famous, Gladys Cooper among them, were bursting into advertising and making large sums (it was always said that the royal family had to do a deal with the proprietors of Pond's Cream when Princess Marina, impoverished and cheerfully and profitably exposing her beautiful face to the soft smoothness of

64

Pond's, became engaged to Prince George). Willie said that he had been approached several times to advertise this or that. Why, then, had he refused? 'To put it bluntly, they've never offered me enough money. I've never done it before and virginity is v-v-v-valuable.' Very occasionally past regrets surfaced. 'Through diffidence or shyness, I've missed a number of chances of sexual congress, even when they were handed to me on a plate.' The combination of the slight pomposity of 'sexual congress' with the slang of 'on a plate' was very characteristic. The age, sex and nationality of the plate-profferers were not produced. He never liked his novels or plays or short stories to be referred to too directly, but an oblique reference, when talking of something else, did not come amiss.

He was immensely kind to the young writers who sent their work to him and asked for advice. He came down to lunch one day, exhausted. 'I've spent the entire m-m-morning telling polite fibs to people I d-d-don't know. I can't h-h-help putting myself in their shoes. When I was young, nobody ever b-b-bothered to encourage me. I only wish the silly b-b-buggers wouldn't write so much.' In Cambridge, at a party for some intelligent undergraduates in King's, he became nervous. 'D-d-d-don't leave me', he whispered, and so I hung about. A highish-minded young man came up and asked him whether he had allowed his stories to be made into films because he 'approved of the cinema as a medium', or some such. Willie became flustered and unhappy. 'Oh, no. I don't give a d-d-d-damn about that sort of thing. I just did it for the m-m-m-m-money.' The undergraduate, looking slightly shocked, walked away. 'I felt I h-h-h-had to tell him the t-t-truth.'

In London, at lunch at the Dorchester, he had just received a fan letter from T. S. Eliot, who had also sent him, and it was January, two dozen red roses ('I feel not unlike an elderly t-t-tart'). Recently, Willie had been to Buckingham Palace to receive from the Queen the considerable honour of the C.H. Of course one congratulated him but, though not ungrateful, he was unimpressed. 'But don't you see what the C.H. means for somebody like me? It means "well done, but . . ." '. He was, of course, referring to the possibility of the O.M., which some, including myself, might consider that he had deserved, an opinion strengthened by a glance at the names of some of the recipients over the last 50 years. But enormous commercial success consorts ill with the O.M. Those aiming at this distinction must be careful not to bring too much enjoyment to too many people.

Tweet Tweet

We all have, I feel sure, a favourite line, good or bad as the case may be, culled from our rich and lavishly varied heritage of English Literature, in which I include, as will be seen, all literature written in English. Regular readers, geared to expect from me nothing but valuable profundities and that serious and sensible approach to life that marks the thinking and 'deeply committed' man, will find me for once in frivolous vein for my own favourite line comes from the treasured *oeuvres* of an American, none other than Ella Wheeler Wilcox. It is a line of verse from a poem which I once knew by heart, and it is, indeed, on my memory that I must now rely as I am currently away from home and there isn't, alas, always room in one's hand-luggage for the complete works of Miss Wheeler Wilcox, though of course I pop them in when space allows.

The narrator of this particular poem is a husband who, after the dinner part of what is clearly being a successful dinner party and while his wife (described as being 'stately', not a very *troublant* adjective) and 'the tenor, McKee' are entertaining the guests in the drawing-room with a 'blithe duet', lights up a fag and, in its fragrant smoke clouds, lets his thoughts wander back to his harum-scarum bachelor days abroad and to the flashing eyes and friendly ways of a dusky female charmer encountered in, if I've remembered correctly, somewhere that sounds suspiciously like Port Said. What actually went on between them? Ah, if only we knew! Despite being the authoress of *Poems of Passion* (1883), our poetess is never one for full frontal information, though she does refer to the episode having occurred during 'days when life was a gay masked ball, and to love and be loved was the sum of it all'. An amorous coupling seems, on the available evidence, a near probability. The recollection is, anyhow, a bitter-sweet one, emotions are stirred, a nostalgic longing for dear, dead moments of the past sweeps over the narrator and he starts quietly to blub. His stately wife spots the tears, stops singing (one can almost hear the guests' sighs of relief) and comes sympathetically over to ask her husband what the matter is. Her choice of words for this solicitous inquiry is *'Qu'avez-vous, dearest, your lids are wet?'* It is the combination of the frog phrasette and the word 'lids' that gets me.

The wife's Christian name is, incidentally, Maud, an unusual one at the present time but by no means the only Maud to grace poetical pages and provide a real cornucopia of handy rhymes ('bored', 'snored', 'gnawed', 'fraud', not that Tennyson goes in for any of them, making do splendidly without). His poem, 'Maud', contains a real conundrum, or rather a brace of conundra over which poetry buffs may be able to help me. No room here for outlining the poem's plot, such as it is. To work! The trouble begins with the poet's almost unbridled enthusiasm for Maud. Sixteen years old precisely (a bit ancient for those child-worshipping Victorians but doubtless they made do with the material available), and socially okay, she is a 'milk-white faun' and 'the delight of the village, the ringing joy of the Hall'. She is, furthermore and unfortunately, 'the moon-faced darling of all'. Be that as it may, Miss Moon Face falls, happily, for the humbly born poet and while she is away from home chatting with him in 'our wood', gathering lilies and getting her slender hand chastely kissed, she is missed up at the Hall.

> Birds in the high Hall-garden
> When twilight was falling,
> Maud, Maud, Maud, Maud
> They were crying and calling.

There now, whatever can one make of that? As to exactly why the birds were crying 'Maud', your guess is as good as mine. A 'Hall' implies a largish garden, complete with both vegetable and fruit areas. Can it be that Maud, anxious to preserve, in two senses, her ripe raspberries, had firmly netted them in and the birds' cry was therefore one of reproach? Or had Maud, with so much on her mind (well, re-read the poem), forgotten to put out their daily portion of nutritious 'Swoop' and the cry was merely one of hunger? The vulgar explanation that the 'birds' to which the poet refers were, in fact, saucy village maidens hanging about in the shadows under the pleached limes for who knows what purpose involving absent, moon-faced Maud, can, in the case of this poet laureate anyway, be at once discounted.

So much for problem number one. Problem number two is, if

anything more baffling. Down in Devon, in the spacious grounds of 'Myrtlebank', our feathered friends are no strangers to us. They twitter me awake and all day long they come and go at will, making, when they feel so disposed, noises, but never a sound have I heard that bears the very faintest resemblance to the name 'Maud'. I have, plainly, been listening to the wrong birds and so, keen as ever to enlarge my horizons of knowledge, I have been poring over the four volumes of Swaysland's *Familiar Wild Birds*, tastefully illustrated and many of which (Bramblings, Little Stints, Water Rails, Creepers, Siskins) are very far from being familiar to me. Certain of W. Swaysland's specimens can be immediately dismissed from the ranks of those capable of chirping out 'Maud'. The Cole Tit, for example. 'This bird makes no pretentions to vocal proficiency. Its note sounds very much like the syllables "che-chee, che-chee" and when sitting in its nest it makes, if molested, an unpleasant hissing noise suggestive of snakes.' Obviously, there is never going to be a 'Maud' here, nor a Guevara for that matter, and it would be charitable to assume that this bird is attempting to offset the unpleasant visual effect of the hissing by forming with its beak the word 'cheese'. Then there is the Redstart which, though 'its haunts are even near to dwelling-houses' (a Hall, for instance), will monotonously keep on going 'chippoo', which gets us nowhere. When thoroughly bored with 'chippoo' it switches to 'oichit' – equally useless.

The Great Tit may sound promising but in spite of occasionally demonstrating intelligence by tapping on beehives to excite the inhabitants and lure a tasty, honey-drenched bee out of doors and down the throat, it falls down completely when it comes to vocalising ('Pinker, pinker, pinker'). And just as hopeless are the crossbill ('Chip, chip, chip'), the kestrel (a disagreeable querulous screaming), the yellow-hammer ('Chit-chit-chirrr'), the chiff chaff ('Chiff chaffy' when pleased: 'whoo-it' when grumpy) and the dunlin ('Kwee-kwee').

There is a possible explanation, if a not very engaging one. One of the many tricks in nature's amorous battery is to make those besotted with another human being fancy that they keep seeing or hearing the loved one when he or she is not at the moment there (how many of us have jumped off buses and darted up side-streets in pursuit of the loved object, only to be confronted by a total stranger, looking cross). At a distance and in a wind, the imprecise monosyllable 'Maud' might sound like almost any other monosyllable, like the noise made by rooks, for instance. The *high* Hall-garden, you note. It contained a rookery, no doubt. Rooks go 'craaw' quite a lot. A love-crazed poet could easily hear it as 'Maud'. Not a very attractive bird, I'm afraid, but moon-faced milkwhite fauns can't have everything.

Spill The Beans

Those for whom death is no longer a very distant landmark (and I can assure you that, even nearing 67, one becomes a pinch thoughtful from time to time) must take care not to remove with them, when their time comes, any valuable piece of information that they could, so easily and profitably, have offloaded onto friends earlier on, causing both gratitude and raised eyebrows. And not only valuable information either. What's wrong with amusing or entertaining or startling items of information? My advice is to scrutinise memory's tablets forthwith for interesting scraps and shed them now while there is time.

My life seems to have been full of people who have withheld from me fascinating facts. It was years, far too many years, before Noël Annan thought to tell me that, as a boy at Stowe, he had become, very rightly and understandably, badly smitten with the exotic charms of a well known film actress from the inscrutable east and called Anna May Wong. He had written a fan letter to her from school (a frivolous sort of activity that would have been much frowned on at Oundle, our record on the rugger field, so incontestably superior to that of Stowe, proving the soundness of our views in this, and other, matters) and he had in due course received by way of reply a happy snap of the celluloid enchantress. And what is more she had kindly signed it 'Orientally Yours, A. M. Wong'. This happening was just a tiny fragment of life's jig-saw, I know, but I resented the wasted decades when I could have been enjoying this little human tit-bit of news.

Then there was a schoolboy called Midgley to whom I taught French in 1933 and who waited till 1958, if you please, by which time he was a father twice over, to inform me that his mother had gone down in the *Titanic*, his very presence there before me indicating that she had successfully come bobbing up again and had subsequently married. To have known this in 1933 would have considerably enlivened our oral French lessons: '*Que fit le grand bateau? Il plongea jusqu'au fond de l'océan. Que fit la mère de*

*. . . to parcel the victims up and then deposit them in the left luggage
departments of railway stations*

Midgley? Elle nagea courageusement.' Apart from anything else, the exercise in the use of verbs ending in *-ger* would have been useful.

And now here we are, well into 1977, before a friend of nearly 30 years' standing and now doing splendidly in Independent Television, decides to write and tell me, doubtless sparked off by my passing reference a week or so ago to Dr Crippen, that his father, an Irish high-church parson, lived in 1909-1910 actually next door to what he describes as 'that respectable medical man' in Hilldrop Crescent, N7, and, what is more, 'liked him very much'. This was of course at the very time when Crippen was planning his unusual course of action over the future of his wife. I think I referred to the good doctor as 'shoddy and inefficient', a description which the facts still seem to bear out, but my friend is clearly anxious to emphasise the then social acceptability of that now somewhat rundown neighbourhood and to demonstrate that somebody at least thought well of the little man. But then clergymen *have* to like people. It's in their contract.

To be, admittedly at third hand but by such a strange chance, once again in touch, more or less, with Crippen, gives one an eerie sensation, although the past is sometimes nearer than we think. We are, after all, only 15 coronations (followed by some shortish reigns) from Elizabeth I, and about 70 generations from Christ. Not very much really. The Twenties and Thirties seem remote in the extreme but in actual fact they are not and, in addition to their other bizarre features, they were above all jammed with sensational murders. The South Coast was then a perilous place for lonely spinsters with nest-eggs. Handsome male rotters picked them out and then picked them up and then picked them off like sitting partridges. What further surprises of a Crippen nature are my friends going to spring on me? Am I going to find that the Bultitudes took a holiday bungalow on the Crumbles at Eastbourne in the very same week in 1924 that Miss Emily Beilby Kaye, with £700 tucked away, fixed up a Crumbles *nid d'amour* with a fiend in attractive human shape called Patrick Mahon? She had, it is true, made most of the running and therefore had only herself to blame, a fact which perhaps provided some morbid consolation when her paramour briskly set about her with an axe. Am I now to discover that Mrs Bultitude, running up a few drop scones next door, heard Miss Kaye's screams but 'didn't like to say anything'?

It seems to me curious that proximity to the sea should so often have caused murderous intent and with it an inclination to parcel the victims up, either whole or in part, and then deposit them in the left luggage departments of railway stations. Mahon recklessly darted up to London with a full Gladstone bag, left it at Waterloo, where, in the exceptionally clement weather, it soon announced its presence, and, madly calling for it a few weeks later (why?), was instantly arrested. Exactly ten years later, a Brighton left luggage attendant became aware of a sizeable canvas suitcase, subsequently found to be containing a female torso, while on the same day among the King's Cross left luggage there turned up a couple of feminine legs. A month or so later, again in Brighton, the police found a large black trunk with, this time, treasure trove in the shape of an entire identifiable corpse in it. And meanwhile up in Scotland a Dr Ruxton had neatly parcelled up various component parts of Mrs Ruxton but, there being unfortunately no railway station conveniently close and with a left luggage section, had had to make other arrangements.

It was almost as if the popular seaside resorts vied with each other. Bournemouth, not to be outshone, produced a murderous chauffeur who, by means of bogus advertisements, enticed superior lady cooks down from London and then, after what cannot have been very satisfactory amorous activities, dispatched them to heaven in a muddy field. Then it was Yarmouth's turn (a woman strangled with a bootlace on the beach), while Charing Cross Station cloakroom provided yet another whiffy black trunk with attendant corpse. Shortly after, the Blackpool sandhills produced a dead body (female, as usual) and the balmy air of Babbacombe brought with it a murdered housewife, done in by a male servant. And where do you suppose that George Joseph (Brides in the Bath) Smith staged those unfortunate accidents? Why, at Weymouth, Herne Bay and Blackpool.

Between 1900 and 1929, 651 men were convicted of murder and were sentenced to death. Of their victims, 536 were adult women, a fact which in those days was considered extremely shocking but would seem less so in this era of women's lib. They are now, presumably, wishful to take murder on the chin along with the male rest of us.

Oh I Say Thanks Awfully

Like many another loyal subject, I have kept by me the official list of the wedding gifts displayed to the public at St. James's Palace on the occasion of the marriage of HRH The Princess Elizabeth to Lieutenant Philip Mountbatten, RN, in November 1947, and now, on this happy Jubilee occasion, I have taken to wondering how they (the gifts) have been getting on. What, for example, of the 'dagger in beaded sheath', the 17 sets of doilies, the 'magic gem of the Orient' and the 'hand-made model of a cat', not to speak of the happy snap of the Dionne Quintuplets, kindly sent along by the Dionne Quintuplets? Presumably the 10 lbs of icing sugar, the turkey, the 4 dozen tins of salmon and the 500 cases of tinned pineapple have long since gone down the royal red lanes.

I had previously understood that it was not permissible to send presents to royalty and that they were always politely returned but I was evidently wrong. The more the merrier seems to have been the motto (there were 2,583 in all) and if I had sent in half a dozen egg cosies and three boxes of Turkish Delight, they would clearly have been acceptable. The skies opened and presents simply showered down. There is really only one way to describe the actual listing of the gifts. Higgledy-piggledy. Perhaps the descriptions of the offerings and the names of the donors were noted down just as they happened to turn up.

The gifts from the King and Queen and fellow royalties certainly appear first on the list and contain some surprises. We find that 45 'members of the royal family', including the Princess Royal and the King of Norway, clubbed together, if you please, and came through with nothing but a mahogany breakfront bookcase. A handsome one, I don't doubt, but surely not quite enough from such a large and rich team. Queen Mary, then pretty long in the tooth, provided 20 assorted gifts off her own bat. Was she, as people of her age often do, off-loading? 'A Chinese screen and a miniature bookcase' sound like things that have been cluttering up the place and collecting dust for years

74

and can now be got rid of. One of the Queen's presents to her daughter was toast-racks (just like you and me, you see), and though the King's present of 'a pair of guns' might cause anxious looks and raised eyebrows in lower strata of society, they are of course perfectly OK in a world where people like going bang-bang on the moors and need to have something to boom off with.

From the general public there were, naturally, duplications, it not having been possible to issue, as many ordinary families do, a list of acceptable presents to intending donors. There were also

Gifts, the usefulness of which is not immediately apparent

frequent multiplications, for example 14 prayer books, 22 bibles, 11 car rugs, 13 wedding cakes, 105 embroidered cloths (table, tea or tray), 156 handkerchiefs, and silk nightdresses galore. Strangest of all were the numbers of people, 74 of them, who felt called upon to send pairs of nylon stockings, one individual donor coughing up as many as 18. They provided between them 159 pairs. Whatever would Freud have to say to that?

Some items might be listed as 'Gifts, the usefulness of which is not immediately apparent'. 'Two collapsible umbrellas' are all right, provided collapsible means folding, but where to find in one's house the absolutely right spot for 'an aboriginal letter in carved wood', a wading stick, a pair of baby clogs, a Basuto bride's charm, 'an inscribed glass shrine on a marble base', and, most difficult to place,' a paraphrase of the 23rd Psalm, mounted under glass', of all psalms the one that would least benefit from paraphrasing. And how on earth would a lady-in-waiting write to express grateful thanks for 'a reversible doll', a hurricane pipe, a gold bicycle mascot and 'a miniature harp in bog oak'? ('Her Royal Highness has asked me to thank you for the miniature harp in, if we mistake not, bog oak.')

There ought really to have been a prize for the most bizarre gift. High in the ratings would have been 'a hide mounted barometer, slung to hang in stirrup'. Stirrups to me mean horses and so what could be handier? The Princess, out riding and worried about the weather, has merely to dismount and take a swift dekko at the forecast. There was also 'a leather mounted calendar', similarly stirrup hung, so she could ascertain the date as well. Then there were 'two harmstrings from Uganda'. Whatever can harmstrings be? They don't sound like good news to me. I misread them first as 'hamstrings', items which must nowadays, sadly, be in all too full supply. Treasured and unique possessions came flooding in and all animal lovers will rejoice to find 'collar of the dog "Patty", the only British survivor of the Kabul massacre in 1879'. Quaint but interesting are 'a truncheon made from laburnum grown in Northern Ireland' and 'writing table accessories made from coal and decorated with nails from the shoes of the Princess's ponies'. And for an appetising, late post-theatre snack, how about raiding the larder for that 'piece of condensed soup' part of the stores in HMS Victory at the Battle of Trafalgar'? Just heat through in a saucepan, toss in a few croûtons, and bring to table.

Things of the mind and books were by no means neglected and, anyway, they had to fill up that mahogany breakfront book-case of which we spoke (and which still seems pretty mingy). The

Aberdovey Women's Institute, whose anxious discussions one likes to imagine, sent along a copy of Berta Ruck's 'Tomboy in Lace', while Mrs St Aubyn Ratcliffe provided her very own 'Furry Folk and Fairies', and two editions of it, what's more. Indeed, the number of writers who decided to conquer their diffidence and bravely send in their own works is really very startling. There were as many as 56 of them, their donations and subjects covering a very wide field: 'Elephants Never Forget', 'The Medical Discoveries of Edward Bach', 'Ballet Education', 'Wedding Etiquette Complete', 'You and the Jury', 'The Finding of the Third Eye' and other treats that one rather doubts ever got very deeply dipped into.

Now, what would one have welcomed most oneself? Well, there were 12 bottles of sloe gin, six of ordinary, a bottle of rum and about a roomful of champagne. There were boxes of chocs and superb silver, glass, furniture and carpets. There was, touchingly, a bunch of violets. But the list is chiefly remarkable for the enormous number of objects which I really feel that I can rub along without: a plastic cushion, 43 lengths of tweed, 'a match holder in the form of a toadstool mounted with a silver frog' (a gift dreamt up by a very close descendant of the last Czar of all the Russias), five copies of a book called 'Daily Light', 'a shaped plastic table' (whatever can an unshaped table look like?), an oil painting of Leeds (a daunting subject until we discover that Leeds is a horse), a 'red velvet vestette', which I take to be a tiny waistcoat, a handmade figure of a coolie, one of Queen Victoria's slippers, a pair of 'Watajoy' travelling bags, a Tibetan incense burner, a bottle of Australian claret, a stinkwood chest, a pink satin suspender belt, 39 Loyal Addresses, a 'yellow hand-painted umbrella' and an ostrich egg.

This Little Pig

Two quite recent examples of unmarried gentlemen coming all too far out into the open and parading before us details of their sexual encounters, 'pleasant or unpleasant as the case may be', make one really wonder whether it's wise for anybody at all to get up to such tricks. For one thing, the writers who indulge in these revelations usually appear to be enjoying themselves and when a writer is enjoying himself, it may be safely assumed that nobody else is. And for another thing, sexual episodes that belong to others are a dead bore from the start. In this modern, flinch-proof world the actual gymnastics, either straight or crooked, shock no more in a book. But time was when they had to be camouflaged. Years ago one had to be alert to discover what was going on. 'And that night, in the humble wayside hotel in the hollow below Spume Tor, Maud and I made sweet music' was the sort of thing one used to read in autobiographical volumes hot from Boots' Library. One skilfully inferred from the words that they meant something more fundamental than a tuneful get-together round the hotel harmonium. And then, and worst of all, writers who go in for this sort of activity instantly lose whatever senses of humour they may once have possessed. The laughs, and there are plenty, are unintentional.

Nobody in this field made a bigger ass of himself than dreadful Frank Harris (is it still remembered that he deflowered Enid Bagnold in, if I remember rightly, a private apartment in the upper regions of the Café Royal? Our informant was the witty and courageous lady herself). His real speciality, however, was the seduction of servant girls, who at first put up a show of modesty when he started what they referred to as messing about ('Now, now, Mr Curious!') but were, according to him, soon swept away by his charms ('I tore off my boots and joined her between the sheets'). And oh dear me, the bosoms and the sighs and the bulges and the thighs. How on earth can somebody write ' "Away with this naughty chemise," I cried, "Beauty must unveil"',' and expect serious attention? No, it really won't do at all and intending sex autobiographers must put away both their egos and their pens.

It seems, however, that we are all at some sort of risk of unconsciously revealing our sexual selves. Even down here at Appleton I now realise that danger lurks. My information comes from the New World and from a somewhat unusual book called *The Sex Life of the Foot and Shoe* by William A. Rossi (published over here by Routledge & Kegan Paul at £4.75). The chapter headings alone spark off a number of new thoughts: 'Sex Symbols at Your Feet', 'Pedic Sadomasochism', 'Cinderella Was a Sexpot', 'Bisexual Shoes', 'Thank Your Foot for Sex', and so on. Incidentally, any similarity with any other Feet is quite unintentional.

Mr Rossi kicks off extremely strongly. 'The foot is an erotic organ and the shoe is its sexual covering.' There now! What unsettling facts to assimilate so late in life. 'Podoerotica' is, it seems, everywhere, even in Devon, but nowhere more so than in the States.

Americans, we are told, consume a billion new shoes a year and 80 per cent of them are purchased with sexual attraction in mind. Reading all this, goggle-eyed, I felt that it wouldn't be too long before dusty old Havelock Ellis popped up his hoary old head and here he is as early as page 2, chipping in with a claim that both foot and shoe are forms of erotic symbolism, upon which I peer nervously down at my comfy 'Norvic' black leather

What to make of my Cousin Madge's wellies?

outdoor shoes from the Army & Navy Stores, size nine, five years old and wearing splendidly. And hard on H. Ellis's heels comes a Mr Rudolfsky who states that 'the word "Feet" is often used as a euphemism for the genitals'. One can only relate such startling statements to one's own world. Strolling down a muddy Devon lane on a damp day and encountering the Bultitudes swinging along on one of their invigorating walks, whatever am I to think when Mrs Bultitude informs me that the upper stream has over-flowed its banks and that she and the Colonel have got their feet wet? Furthermore, she adds that they are both exhausted and that, when they get in, they are jolly well going to put their feet up.

Selfless Mr Rossi has visited, on our behalf, no fewer than 25 countries, inspecting shoes and feet in all directions. In dreary old London he claims to have discovered a Palace of Pedic Plea-sure, its clientèle entertained by mobile ladies with mobile feet (directions are vague but at a guess it's somewhere near Whiteley's) and goodness me, the assorted items of news that he provides! For example, on America's West Coast 'toe movies' are to be seen. The big toe is a phallic symbol and in Middle Europe they apparently anoint it with a mixture of vegetable oil and Spanish fly, hoping for beneficial results in other quarters.

Treat corns and bunions with beef suet laced with frankincense or, even better, asses' urine mixed with mud (recipes by courtesy of Pliny the Elder, A.D. 79). A Milwaukee shoe company asserted that their shoes relieved insomnia, constipation, eczema, catarrh and nervous indigestion. American foot fetishists can now either join the Lotus Love Foot Erotica Club or, more elaborately, stump up $30 to a dial-an-obscene-talk phone service (two 15-minute calls a week permitted to each paid-up member, and no subjects barred). A New York shoe firm advertises a scent called *Fleurs de Feet* (apply to the instep). Oddest of all among Mr Rossi's dis-coveries is the fact that King Victor Emmanuel II of Italy cut his big toe (!) nails once a year, had them framed in gold and en-crusted with diamonds, and presented them ('Now Victor, you're spoiling me!') to his mistresses, as 'memen-toes' merrily quips Mr Rossi in one of his fortunately few unbuttoned moments.

The whole book has put me into a thoroughly jumpy state. What now to make of my Cousin Madge's stout brogues, let alone her wellies? If I spot Miss Entwhistle coming out of Matins and sporting 3-inch stilettos, am I really to think, as Mr Rossi would have me do, that she is 'subconsciously trying to "stab" back at men in a male-dominated world'? When the summer comes, and the Bultitudes kindly allow us all to splash about in their heated pool ('Drinks under the cedar, everybody. Just *helpez-vous-mêmes!*'), how on earth am I to stop gazing, mesmerised, at the Colonel's big toes or keep myself from wondering whether Mrs Bultitude has recently anointed them? And I begin to wish that Mr Rossi hadn't told me that a pair of feet contains 120,000 sweat glands. But despite the Pedic Palace, Mr Rossi's opinion of our 'native footwear styles' is extremely poor. He finds them 'dull, sterile, unimaginative and reflecting a definitely lower level on the sociosexual thermometer.'

And I should hope so too.

Don't Forget to Write

In my agreeable circle of Devonian friends and relations, centred on our picturesque little village of Appleton, we are all great postcard senders. Apart from cheques, few communications are pleasanter to find in the morning's mail. They give brief news, they feast the eyes and they require no answer. My Cousin Madge wouldn't dream of making one of her adventuresome trips without sending me an informative coloured p.c., even if her destination is somewhere as relatively near-at-hand as Weston-Super-Mare (by which they really mean Weston-Super-Bristol Channel – well, look at the map). Miss Entwhistle's bi-annual visits to Scarborough, which by our Appleton standards put her firmly in the globetrotting category, result in a shower of heartening Views jammed with excited scribbles outlining her doings. The Bultitudes' postcards tend, of course, to come from smart foreign parts and kindly unbend to our level ('We think you'd enjoy this amusingly grubby little *hôtel*'). It is Mrs Bultitude who takes care of the epistolary side of this happy and productive union (three sturdy youngsters, now grown up and fled the cosy nest) but, when it comes to sticking on stamps, Mrs Bultitude is, I am sorry to report, nothing but slapdash. No neat alignment. No head the right way up. For a French *timbre* or a German *Briefmark,* any position at all will plainly 'do'. Who, after all, won the war, may one ask?

It is perhaps just as well for her and the Colonel's peace of mind that she clearly knows nothing of a French postcard called *Langage du Timbre* ('*La position du timbre exprime le désir secret du coeur*'). It features a lovesick frog pair, entwined in a sea of tastefully tinted pansies (those flowers that are 'for thoughts') with, all around them, drawings of stamps stuck on crooked and the secret meaning contained in each lopsided position. Thus, when Mrs B greets our vicar from afar with the harbour at Cannes by moonlight and off-handedly tilts her *timbre* to the left, she is saying *'Je vous adore!'* A hasty p.c. to the milkman, asking him to start up his lactic visits again on the 10th, with the stamp upside-down and crooked at that, says, as plain as plain, *'Aimez-moi toujours!'* I myself have in the past received from her the Opera House at Milan ('Blotti in great voice last night') with the *timbre* or, in this case, *franco-bollo*, lying down sideways and signifying *'Je reste fidèle'*, which I can only hope means *fidèle* to the Colonel.

Our knowledge of postcard history (they began in America in 1861) is enormously increased, thanks to Jupiter Books and at a cost of £5.50, by witty Alan Wykes and his splendidly illustrated *Saucy Seaside Postcards*. One's thoughts fly at once to the famous artist, Donald McGill, originator of that classic example of parental distress ('I've lost my Little Willie') and here is, among many others, his story and majestic reproductions of his output. Ill-rewarded (at first he got an outright payment of 6/- a card, and as a result died leaving merely a few hundred) and infinitely respectable, he relished the pleasing fact that at the old boy dinners of his public school he was always put next to the Bishop of Wakefield. In this field, respectability does win occasionally through (Blackpool, of all places, has been known to sniff disapprovingly at certain jokes, prior to banning them. Whatever can they have been?) and what goes well at Llandudno may be frowned on frostily at Lowestoft, but by and large the merriments of nudist clubs (usually called either the Snogmoor or the Koolbums) are universally popular, together with chamber-pots, Scotsmen's kilts and the mysteries that lie beneath, wedding nights, a pint beer tankard with a smiling face on it ('I shall be glad to see your jolly old mug again') and an enormously stout lady tumbling, in a shower of boulders, down a cliffside ('I've fallen in a big way for a boy down here') with a great display of knickers. McGill, naturally.

One has, of course, one's favourites. I particularly like the two tipsy gentlemen strap-hanging in the Underground and the dialogue that accompanies it: 'Is this Wembley?' 'No, it's Thursday.' 'So am I. Let's have another drink.' And there is the man giving helpful information to a distraught lady hunting her missing cat which has taken refuge beneath a small car ('Miss Cox, I can see a little fluffy thing under your mini'). There is also an hysterical male hospital patient flying half-clothed and in great disarray down a corridor pursued by a muddle-headed nurse holding a steaming saucepan, while a doctor chides her with 'No, no, Nurse Duncan, I said prick his boil.' Get it? All simple fun, here excellently assembled and paraded.

The slightly less saucy and more basic side of our investigations

Naked statues were Art and Art was perfectly all right

is much assisted by *Erotic Postcards*, the thoughtful work of Barbara Jones and William Ouellette (Macdonald and Jane's: £4.95) and it is brimful with illustrations of the many treats of yesteryear. When, a few years ago, almost every bookstall and paper-shop in the land started to provide magazines featuring bold ladies defiantly displaying their vast busts (big is beautiful, it seems, in the chest world), the day of the erotic, and publicly saleable, postcard was finally over, and we can here discover what we're now missing. Cheer up. It doesn't really amount to very much. Our grandfathers appear to have been fairly easily stimulated – scantily dressed actresses dangling pairs of cherries from pearly teeth and looking roguish, ladies rigged up in military uniform and symbolising discipline by cracking whips in a menacing manner, unbridled apache dancers throwing each other violently about, and seaside fisherwomen bending over the better to scoop up shrimps on a blustery day and affording a generous eyeful of bloomer for male strollers along the promenade.

There were accepted rules about nakedness. Models stripped off, donned white body stockings and pretended to be statues. Naked statues were Art (even Queen Victoria was known to gaze admiringly at statues) and Art was perfectly all right. Muscular and fig-leaved men were allowed to present themselves publicly provided they were personifying something respectable such as Agriculture or Peace or Industry or Plenty. There were, inevitably, numerous photographs of the famous and notorious – a semi-draped Mata Hari taking time off from her sketchy cloak and dagger commitments and about to go into her undulating *Danse Indienne* (there is another snap of her improbably disguised as a nun). And there was La Belle Otero, by far the most successful courtesan of the last century (her clients were almost exclusively crowned heads, our own deplorable old Edward among them), who died penniless in Nice at the age of 97 and in the very act of preparing a rabbit stew. What a lesson for the immodest!

A final dazzling pictorial round-up, darting from one fascinating book to the other, produces aquatic fun in the pool ('May I splash you in the deep end?'), huge bare ladies stuck in the doors of bathing-machines, shameless *Françaises* eating jumbo asparagus in a provocative manner, robust girls climbing trees or being peered at through key-holes or getting tied up or spanked. There are frilly garters galore and harem inmates and wet lower lips and enormous pink behinds and mishaps on bicycles and a double meaning whichever way you turn. There is nothing here nowadays to shock, unless it be the ugliness and the vulgarity and, throughout, the total lack of wit, apart from that kindly supplied by the good Mr Wykes and his fellow-researchers.

The Tall Gentleman

When I am fortunate enough to have visitors staying with me in Devon, they are usually kind enough to accompany me on a leisurely stroll through the orchard to our spacious and splendidly stocked village shops (we have, surprisingly, three of them). American visitors especially find the goods therein displayed, and the people purchasing them, an interesting sight and so when a married couple from Wisconsin came to stay with me in 1972, it was to these shops that one morning we made our way – a tall gentleman, a less tall lady, and me. We went into our nearest all-purpose grocery and were examining the range of biscuits on a shelf hard by the jams and pickles section when I felt a tug at my elbow. There was nice Mrs Harding, late of London and in her day a great theatre-goer (we play dear old 78s together and bemoan the arrival of the kitchen sink). 'Excuse me, but isn't that tall gentleman Alfred Lunt?' It was a proud moment. 'Yes, it is,' I said. 'And of course Lynn Fontanne?' 'Yes indeed. The Lunts.' I feel as happily boastful now as I felt happily boastful then. That's what contact with greatness does for some of us. Forgive it, and remember that if God himself came down on earth and had a chat with you while you were thinning out your lettuces. the first thing that you would want to do later would be to fly off and brag about it to your chums ('But I tell you, Enid, He was *there*!').

They were certainly Gods to me. I first saw them in *Caprice*, a thinnish piece as the title implies, at the St James's Theatre, London, in 1929. For years the stage had had an accepted style of comedy acting. An actor would come to the end of a speech and then it was, so to speak, somebody else's turn to talk. No performer would dream of starting up until another had finished (it worked all right – think of *The Importance of Being Earnest*). The Lunts turned all this topsy-turvy. They spoke as people do in life. They overlapped each other, they threw away lines, they trod on words, they whispered, they shouted, and from this realistic jumble (have you ever heard a recording of a dinner party conversation? Everybody yells and nobody ever finishes a sentence) the essentials emerged. And they had in addition enormous elegance and charm and, in Lynn's case, great beauty ('I wasn't much to look at when I was young,' she once said, 'but I got a little better as time went on'). Between them, they dazzled and glittered and high comedy acting has never been the same since.

I first met them, as indissoluble then as they still are now, even though death has had a go at separating them, in London during the war. They had arrived from America very courageously via Lisbon and the dangerous air passage which had already cost the life of Leslie Howard. They were shortly to open in *There Shall Be No Night*. I was goggle-eyed with excitement and admiration (the 1930s had brought us *Reunion in Vienna* and *Amphitryon 38*). They could clearly recognise a demented fan when they saw one and they were very kind and understanding. Lynn's beautiful hair was arranged in two large and lustrous swags, if that be the word, with a bunch of fresh violets tucked in between them.

She wondered if they needed watering. Would I please have a look and perhaps sprinkle a few drops of water on them from time to time. She told me that the sides of their double bed in their hotel were higher than the bit in the middle, which tended to roll them together and that this was much jollier than the converse. She added, *à propos de rien*, that it is extremely difficult to keep up a squabble in a double bed. Alfred asked me if I had ever heard of a famous American actress called Mrs Minnie Fiske, who could be absent-minded. Going once backstage after a first night to congratulate the performers, she entirely forgot the purpose of her visit, opened the dressing-room door of the expectantly waiting leading lady, shouted through it 'Goodnight, goodnight' and, disappearing down the passage, was seen no more. I was their slave from then on.

Alfred was in every way a perfectionist, whether he was cooking or gardening or acting. Taking, with his devoted dresser and friend, Jules, the *cordon bleu* examination in Paris, he had trembled even more violently than on a first night ('I had to ask the lady next to me to switch on my stove'). I doubt if they ever gave a performance in which they did not try to improve something and it was alleged that before the final night of *Love in Idleness*, a company rehearsal was called. I was lucky enough to be allowed to watch them rehearsing this delightful play and to see the elaborate jigsaw of their acting being assembled piece by piece. They repeated a dozen times, and then either rejected or adopted, a bit of stage business that might take only a second to do but which would add point to a line. You may say that this is what all actors do, but it can never have been done with more devotion and dedication and expertness. And, indeed, success. During the actual run of a play, Alfred's performance never satisfied him ('If only you had come *last* night,' he used to wail, 'instead of tonight. I was awful.'). Alfred's pronunciation of 'awful' came out to an English ear as 'offal' and pleased his friends.

Happily staying with them in Alfred's charming old family house near Milwaukee, or in Florida where they sometimes spent the winter, it was delightful to find them still discussing whether, in 1935, it had been right to cut a certain scene in *The Taming of the Shrew*. 'Alfred, I could have got a laugh in that scene.' 'Oh no, Lynnie, no, it was a dull scene and better out of the way.' 'Alfred, there was a *laugh* there . . .': and so on. Entirely modest (their fame meant nothing to them and they seemed to be hardly aware of it), they could not wait, like all the most agreeable actors, to tell of theatrical moments when things had gone wrong.

There was the famous occasion when, on tour, the theatre's stalls had flooded and they had, of course, played on across a sea of water to the upper parts of the house (a lady's flowered hat fell from the dress circle and floated merrily to and fro). There had been the night when, in *Elizabeth the Queen,* Alfred, as Essex, had buried his face too violently in Lynn's generously bejewelled bosom and had broken the strings of her pearls, which shot about all over the stage, one of them becoming embedded in Alfred's nostril. There had been, in New York, the daunting dress rehearsals before the dour and chilly and unsmiling board of the Theatre Guild, whom Alfred addressed at curtain fall ('Playing light comedy to you is like trying to feed a soufflé to a horse').

And how dearly he loved to laugh, and never unkindly – at human oddities and behaviour, at unusual performers (there was a largish cabaret artiste called Miss Baby Dumpling), at TV advertisements (a very English actor unconvincingly rigged up as a guzzling Italian and intoning joyously *'Mamma mia,* was dat a spicy meat-ball!). Nobody enjoyed it more than he when, in the index of a book by Godfrey Winn, he misprintedly appeared as 'Mildred Lunt'. For some time after, he signed his letters 'Mildred'. I can hear him chuckling still.

Take A Pew

Any burglar unwisely planning to force an entry by night into my Devon residence, 'Myrtlebank', and later to make off with my plated cheese scoop, my nest of walnut occasionals and my treasured collection of burnt-poker-work mottoes ('Don't Worry, It Won't Happen'), is in for a double shock. The first will be one of disappointment at the low value set in the open market on my derisory portable possessions (to a lady jumble-sale collector who asked me what I did with my old clothes, I politely replied that I folded them neatly at night and put them on again when it was morning). The second shock, and it is a sharper one, will be the discovery of how alert I am and how well prepared for just such a happening, with my counter-measures at the ready.

Securely locked into my bedroom upstairs (it always amazes me to learn how few people, living alone, take this elementary precaution) and hearing a disturbance below, I instantly leap from bed, rattle back the bedroom curtains, switch on both bedroom lights, fling wide the windows and send peeling out into the night the really deafening sound made by the brass handbell which, in my clerical grandfather's house in North Devon, used to call us all, servants included, to morning and evening prayers (the cheerful summons had to reach the furthest corners of the large garden so that the gardener didn't, in the morning, miss the uplift). I understand that the two things that a nocturnal thief dreads most are, apart from shotguns, noise and light. Not realising how deeply the other Appleton inhabitants sleep and therefore how less than nimbly they will fly to my aid, he will be off through the orchard like a lamplighter, shedding my mottoes as he goes ('Be Like The Kettle, Up To Its Neck In Hot Water But Still Keeps Singing').

The dangers of exposing children to violence and sex on TV are currently being widely discussed but there is really nothing new in this. In my youth there was, naturally, no television but we were exposed daily to something just as crowded with violent

The two things a nocturnal thief dreads most

and unsavoury happenings and sexual deplorablenesses. I am referring, of course, to the Old Testament. When everybody, summoned by the bell, was collected together and soberly seated in my grandfather's study we first plunged forward on to our knees for prayers while my grandmother, through eyes half-open above her folded hands, made sure that everybody was correctly and devoutly at it and praying away like anything. Then, when that was safely over, my grandfather would boom off at us a fiery passage or two from the O.T., pausing here and there to expound or illustrate. Sometimes a door-bell rang, *in mediis rebus,* upon which my mother would jump to her feet and, with a great show of reluctance and self-denial, would hurry out. Her implausible excuse was that she did not want the servants to be disturbed in their devotions but she always broke down badly under any subsequent cross-examination on this point and subsided into giggles.

She was only too right to escape when she could, for what in the meantime was being paraded before us from the good book? Well, wholesale incest to start off with. We'd barely begun on Genesis before Adam's unprincipled son, Seth, begat at the age of 105 a male child most unfortunately called Enos (Enos meant only one thing – a tummy upset and fizzy fruit salts). And begat by whom, may one ask? There was nobody female about but his sisters and even at the age of ten I was aware that that sort of hanky-panky was not to be recommended. I had no sister and so was mercifully free from temptation, but what of the gardener, who was known to have a large sister called Mrs Burnham? He looked innocent enough, sitting there, but were sinful ideas not being put into his head? Enos lived to be 905 and, again making use of extremely close relations (perhaps an aunt or two, for who can tell?), begat several children. And then, before one knew where one was, Noah was filling up that unhygienic ark with members of his family and assorted livestock and one had to try very hard not to think of how perfectly frightful the smells must have been. And after the ark had landed, tremendous inbreeding began all over again. Really very unsatisfactory.

After incest, we passed lightly on, day by day, to almost any other imperfection that you may care to name – rape, murder, torture, slaughter, public stonings, Jezebel reluctantly forming a new brand of tasty dog-food and wily old Onan managing as best he could on his own. My grandfather was a kindly man in many ways who himself lived a life of abstinence and great purity, but perhaps as a result of this he didn't at all mind people getting what was coming to them. There was a chapter which he particularly enjoyed in Deuteronomy when 'the Lord thy God' rattles off a warning list of the physical penalties in this life, and never mind the brimstone later, that can be expected to follow disobedience. There were 57 breath-taking verses and, indeed, 57 varieties of horror, with haemorrhoids and boils (the Egyptian and especially stubborn kind), itches and scabs and mildew and worms in the grapes and locusts all over everything and more boils and more scabs and invasion by a sort of Hitler and, to crown all, cannibalism.

And then, if you please, along came poor old Job, victim of a product-testing survey by the Great Manufacturer, to prove that even if you behaved yourself, you weren't out of the wood yet. There he was, resident in the Land of Uz, wherever that may be, a respected citizen and minding his own business when suddenly his stockbroker announces his portfolio as being valueless, his house is blown down, his sheep struck by lightning, his oxen stolen and his health ruined (boils again) and, the brokers' men having removed the furniture, nothing to perch on but ashes. Most objectionable of all, perhaps, was to be lectured on secret sin by three dreadful friends called Eliphaz, Bildad and Zophar, troublemakers every one of them.

Though none of this was at all agreeable to listen to so soon after breakfast, it didn't really encourage anybody, by example, to rush out and rape the maids or stone the headmaster. It merely filled a youthful mind with astonishment that such dreadful things could be allowed by somebody so all-powerful, apparently. It was the callous cruelty that sickened one. Needless, too, whatever feeble explanations the holy may trump up. However, the empty and echoing churches of today are there to show that, in the end, even He seems to have got what was coming to Him.

Swing Swing Together

A hundred and fifty or so years ago, a public school headmaster busily concocting one of those fraudulently misleading school prospectuses – 'extensive grounds, bathing in "Splosher", tradition-soaked buildings, intellectual and other disciplines inculcated, fine "tone", resident matron, food' – complete with photographs of falsely smiling inmates ('a cheery group on Big Side celebrating "Cuppers" '), would naturally have suppressed what was then one of the very few advantages of four profitless and dangerous years at a boarding school, namely, that it made the whole of the rest of existence thereafter seem by comparison like a prolonged and pleasurable picnic.

A cross-section of experiences of public school life down the centuries leaves one gasping. Ferocious beatings (Winchester thoughtfully experimented with stout apple branches bound together in a two foot holder, but came back in the end to good old birch), up at 5 a.m., Latin and Greek until midday and then a meal of watery gruel and currants (Merchant Taylors' provided no midday food at all until 1870), devilish bullying, 20 days' holiday a year, solitary confinement as a punishment (Christ's Hospital and Mill Hill), headmasters who were wild figures and as ruthless and powerful as Hitler (early ones had the power to excommunicate) and a staff whom the Felsted statutes thought it prudent to specify should not be 'drunkards or whore-hunters'. Dulwich took boarders at the age of four and at Eton the collegers competed for their food with regiments of rats. So much for the *de luxe* view, held by some, of these 'young toffs' ' establishments.

Fifty years ago, conditions had greatly improved and at Oundle I was extremely happy, despite the surprising ups and downs of school life. I was in what was called a 'proprietary' house (the housemaster, conscience-stricken or not, made what profit he could) where we sometimes found ourselves at suppertime staring, ravenous and bemused, at a solitary pilchard perched on a cabbage leaf masquerading as lettuce. For the first two years not a day passed without a Latin lesson and the boredom that went with it. If you were in bad trouble or very unhappy, there was nobody to whom you could conceivably have gone for help, least of all the housemaster (it was then fashionable for them to be entirely remote and unapproachable). If you had explained that you didn't really like rugger or cricket all that much and didn't want to take part and would therefore gladly yield up your place to another, gaining thereby good marks for unselfishness, you would have been instantly thrashed and given a tremendous lecture on 'letting down the house'. Indeed, so geared was I to taking daily exercise in a sort of automaton trance that, on going up to Cambridge I assumed that we all had to play *something* and enrolled myself for hockey. Ribald friends, mocking my post-lunch bicyclings, all kitted up and ready for the fray, down the Huntingdon road, soon put me wise to the fact that exercise and, to a very slightly lesser degree, work, were quite unnecessary and I sawed up and burnt my hockey stick on the fire in my rooms; it made a very disagreeable smell.

The vast past history of public schools, a weird and wonderful phantasmagoria if ever there was one, is now fully and inexhaustibly revealed to us for the first time by Jonathan Gathorne-Hardy (Bryanston and Cambridge) in his *The Public School Phenomenon*, a copy of which, excellently illustrated, Messrs Hodder and Stoughton (say it, apparently, Storton) will cheerfully let you have for £7.50 and which really covers everything. Our author, equipped, and how essentially, with a splendid sense of humour, is particularly strong on just those details that fascinate, and especially on the eccentrics whom such schools have always gathered to their bosoms.

For example, Gill of St Paul's used to rush out and beat old boys who had come down to see the dear old place again, and beat too any passer-by who irritated him. Moss of Shrewsbury found games quite incomprehensible and at football matches used to ask what time stumps were to be drawn. Bradley of Marlborough raced pigeons, often pressing a basket of them on to visitors leaving by train with a request that they open the carriage window and release the birds at Didcot. Braythwaite of Lancing had a belch so violent that it blew his hand away from his mouth when he could get it there in time. The 1742 headmaster of Sedbergh disliked both boys and schools to such an extent that he spent his entire tenure of office firmly locked in his study. The 1818 headmaster of Bromsgrove, on the other hand, liked a more open life and spent nine consecutive days in a public house

Staring, ravenous and bemused, at a solitary pilchard

(asked to leave both the pub and the school). Temple of Rugby sobbed loudly while flogging, a doubly unnerving experience for the floggee. Percival of Clifton insisted on breeches for footer, fearful that the boys might find the sight of each other's knees too unbearably disturbing. Udall, headmaster of Eton until imprisoned for the gravest of sexual misdemeanours, popped up again on his release from choky as headmaster of Westminster in what must have been perhaps a rather lean year. Benson of Wellington climbed about festooning the tops of the dormitory cubicles with barbed wire to discourage informal visiting after lights-out.

Literary figures haven't always made too good a showing at their public schools. Our delightful poet laureate was in ceaseless trouble at Marlborough. L. P. Hartley was 'whopped' at Harrow for leaning too far out of a window on a Sunday. Harold Nicolson found at Wellington that intellectual powers were considered to be in some way effeminate. At Malvern, our much revered ex-literary editor, Raymond Mortimer, was rated a duffer at games and suspended upside down over an unflushed lavatory bowl. Cyril Connolly was given at Eton a beating by the self-elected bloods, an alarmingly powerful super-prefectorial body answerable, apparently, to nobody. Indeed, a feature of the last century (and perhaps of this) is the ease with which masters allowed senior boys to take over the running of the place. At Marlborough, a housemaster was outraged at being disturbed by a prefect who came to announce that the building was on fire ('That's your department!').

Turning Mr Gathorne-Hardy's packed and enthralling pages (478 of them. There's value for you), one can almost smell the damp towels, the soggy socks, the changing room, the doorless lavatories, the prophylactic aroma of Matron's 'den', the scent of cigars and rich foods beyond the baize door that led to more luxurious quarters, and the unforgettable, unforgotten whiff of cabbage cooked without the hand of love.

By no means all boys conformed or stood the pace and there were some brave enough to stage rebellions. Glorious uprisings took place at Eton (harsh conditions: flogging block smashed), Harrow (led by Byron: gunpowder used for the first time), Rugby (for 'Rights of Boys': army brought out), Sherborne (meat gone putrid: all prefects expelled), Marlborough (all privileges removed: fireworks ingeniously used as weapons and damages running into thousands). A very remarkable 15-year-old called Esmond Romilly (a snap of the period shows a finely belligerent face), ran away from Wellington, established himself in London, issued a fiery revolutionary magazine called 'Out of Bounds' and called for representatives from other public schools to voice their grievances. In no time at all, delegates played truant and courageously turned up – Ledward of Charterhouse, Pilkington of Lancing and, another splendid literary person, Philip Toynbee of Rugby, subsequently sacked but with a glowing testimonial for initiative. The revolt fizzled out, but it was a spirited affair while it lasted.

Tolstoy's Aunt on Serious Charge

On the night before my parents' wedding on 19 April (Primrose Day, and my father's birthday), 1906, an unforeseen and world-shattering event took place that must have seemed at the time an extremely ill omen for a placid and contented married life. I am referring, of course, to the great San Francisco earthquake and fire, with the resulting appalling loss of life, the news of which, feverishly reported in the pages of the *Morning Post*, reached them during the first hours of their honeymoon at Lynmouth and provided my mother, I assume, with her second severe shock of the day. But what of the omen? How did things turn out, you ask? Instant separation? Divorce before the year was out? Nothing of the sort. California is a long way from North Devon and the disastrous seismic waves, both actual and psychological, had petered out long before they reached that rocky shore. The marriage was basically a very happy one and it endured, though whether or not my subsequent appearance is also to be considered as a calamitous natural disaster is up to you. Anyway, like it or not, I'm pressing on and I hope to be troubling the Great Scorer for a while yet with a few more wristy snicks through the covers, a leg glide or two to 'point', or whatever seems appropriate.

The year 1906 was full of other, milder surprises, some of them quite pleasant (opening of the Simplon tunnel to railway traffic) and for a heartening *coup d'oeil* at what was afoot one hastens automatically to the bound volumes of that delightful weekly illustrated magazine, *The Sketch*, where one finds oneself instantly knee-deep in crowded happenings, excitements everywhere. Hamburg fire-fighters, we discover, are now zooming into action on motorised tricycles at a speed said to be not far short of 15 m.p.h. The oldest lady in Japan, thought to be at least 110, has been recently provided with a copper ear-trumpet and, misunderstanding its purpose, struck gamely out with it at anybody rash enough to attempt a chat. A Tottenham roadmenders' shelter is being used (and don't ask me why) as a changing-room by lady hockey-players. A vendor of 'revolutionary buttons' (made in Birmingham, it says), has been recklessly vending away in the streets of what was then a pleasingly tolerant St Petersburg, causing raised eyebrows rather than raised fists. A grey-haired Latvian finds his hair turning bright red during moments of emotional disturbance, and a prominent Russian ballerina has sued a quack dimple-cutter for the sum of 1500 roubles for cutting two faulty and subsequently septic dimples in her knees (out of *Swan Lake* for weeks).

With photographic reproduction in newspapers still in its fairly early stages and something of an attractive novelty, almost anything was adjudged to be fully snapworthy. Here, scratching away for dear life and wildly cackling from time to time, is the picked team of loyal Buff Orpingtons who are supplying the Cambridge boatrace crew with eggs (40 required for breakfast alone, if you please, and a real challenge to our feathered friends). There, and how devilishly ingenious it is, is a police speed-trap consisting of a posse of stop-watched bobbies cunningly concealed in a mobile artificial hedge on the Birnam Wood principle. Occasionally one can feast the eyes on a more peaceful subject – Stoke Poges from the south, Chalfont St Giles from the east, Slough at dusk, and 'early morning in the W. H. Smith employees' rest room' (snore, snore) – only to be once more eager and alert to drink in a very sulky looking lady who turns out to be the grumpy Archduchess Clotilde (financially ruined by unwise speculation on the Hungarian *bourse*), together with bold Esther McEwan, a Scottish lassie of 15 who, disguised as a boy, worked in a mine and went on three sea voyages before her sex was discovered. Whether or not she then thought oh what the hell and signed on for a fourth sea voyage we are not told.

Certain of our newspapers, ever anxious to intrigue and stimulate the readers, daily supply information concerning interesting anniversaries. I find it nothing but jolly to learn over the bacon and egg that on this very date 160 years ago Garibaldi went to the dentist for the first time or that in 1861 Tolstoy's aunt was arrested for shoplifting, found guilty and sentenced to 30 whacks with the dreaded knout (I only wish they would try this out in Oxford Street on those middle-eastern ladies who, when apprehended, are found to have £5,894 in their bags). My only difficulty is that I can so seldom remember, even if I ever knew, the precise circumstances of the event selected from history's brimming pages, after who knows what anxious deliberations, for Fleet

Street canonisation. I should, for example, be sorry to be asked, in the general knowledge section of *Mastermind* (specialist subject: English Musical Comedy, 1924-1954), for details of the Diet of Worms, beyond announcing the fact, surely plain to all, that as a collection of words it outstandingly lacks euphonious charm.

Apart from the eleven lovely years of AD 8 to AD 19 (Death of Horace, Death of Ovid, Death of Livy, Death of Virgil, all entirely welcome removals, woefully delayed in some cases and far too seldom celebrated by the *Daily Telegraph*), the anniversaries picked out usually merely make one rather glad, for once, to be in the here and now. Eighty or so years ago, you could hardly hear yourself speak for the din from the loud explosions of infernal machines, busily dispatching various foreign royalties, together with – and what a lesson for rubber-necks – those sometimes referred to as 'curious bystanders'. The Shah of Persia went pop in 1896, ditto King Humbert four years later. The really spectacular assassinations of Czar Alexander II, the King of Portugal (bowling along, carefree as you like, through Lisbon) and King George of Greece were put utterly in the shade, and here the English record is sadly poor, by the entire royal family of Serbia who all went up together in one great big glorious bang. In the middle of all this carnage, the invention of the Remington typewriter provided a sorely needed solace for all.

Perhaps there is, after all, just a little to be said in favour of living round about BC 282 (Death of Euclid). Building was flourishing (the Great Wall of China was going up) and, for excitement and spectacle, the Gauls could always be counted on to turn unexpectedly up and sack something. For lively reading there was the Indian London Library, and the invention of the magnetic needle could tell you how to get there (you could take in the Temple of Luxor on the way). It is true that the sun seems to have eclipsed itself more frequently than it does now, and I dare say the nights were chilly, but with wall to wall rush flooring, all-purpose house-coats in dyed Persian lamb, and handfuls of slow-burning camel's dung thrust into the Kosiglow, one could have made oneself just as snug as snug.

Unholy Ghosts

Among the correspondents who have been kind enough, over the last two years, to write to me about this or that, some of them with envelopes bearing first-class stamps and bringing with them an exciting sense of postal urgency, there have so far been only two crosspatches. One, a man, was vexed that 50 years ago I had saved up a month's pocket money (a working man's weekly wage) and had blued the lot on a matinée of *Mercenary Mary*, with tea in the interval and a box of soft centres. Ah well. The other, a woman and American I would think as, on parting, she signed herself merely 'Sincerely', was distressed that I seemed to speak so lightly of the relative ease with which perfectly sensible women are able to get themselves murdered, tip-toeing as they do trustfully within hatchet-range of obvious rotters, accepting lifts in cars belonging to unknowns ('Drop me at Dedham, if you will'), or swigging down a palpably doctored port-and-lemon ('Cheers!'). All I was doing in this case was attempting politely to point out that women are, plainly, far nicer and more honest and more trusting than men. 'Gullible' isn't, somehow, an agreeable adjective, but that's what they are too. 'Credulous' ditto, and in no field more so than in that of seeing, or thinking to see, ghosts. For every one man who claims to have sighted a spirit, there are five women with weirder, spookier tales to tell.

A case in point. I am sometimes fortunate to have at weekends visiting friends gracing what I like to think of as the West Wing of 'Myrtlebank'. There are just the two rooms there which, if not exactly meriting the hotelier's descriptive word 'luxi-bedrooms', do at least have beds and a full tin of biscuits at the side of them (in most other people's houses, there is practically no single moment of the day or of the night when one can't 'manage' a digestive or a petit beurre). Staying with me last year was a married lady, mother of three and the very soul of level-headedness, or so one would have thought, but she came down to Sunday breakfast (9 a.m., for 9.15. Hot dishes. Preserves) in a state of considerable agitation, announcing that, two minutes before, she had seen a ghost. Swiftly calming her with kedgeree and coffee, I begged her to tell all. Gazing from her bedroom window in the misty Devonian morning light and out over the generously-filled rose beds that lead to the gate, she had seen, she said, a little old white-haired lady come floating up the path and who, passing as though by magic through the solid stone house wall, three feet thick, had vanished from sight within the premises. Should we investigate? What could it mean? A death? A dreadful warning of some kind? Had the ghost ever been seen before?

'Indeed yes,' I explained, 'we see her daily. She is fond of sherry and bananas and she has a light hand with pastry. Your ghost is none other than a delightful and devout little Welsh dumpling called Mabel, an ex-nurse billeted on us in Berkshire during the war and now, in retirement and with her nasal probe and kidney dishes finally hung up, making cosy use of the three rooms, superfluous to my needs, in the East Wing of 'Myrtle-bank'. She was able to pass through the wall because there is a

. . . with soft arms and softer breasts pressed to his canonicals

door there. She has just returned from early service in the village church. Her hair is white because she is 86. Any more questions?'

I do not, mundane and prosaic as I am, much believe in ghosts but I am by no means uninterested in their reported goings-on, in no way astonished to find that the Other Side seems to be every bit as cracked as this. Clergymen, despite that private telephone line to the Great Exchange in the sky, are quite frequently exposed to the most curious and eerie doings. Take, for example, the case of the Rev. Ernest Merryweather, a no-nonsense name if ever there was one, appointed in 1937 to the living of Langenhoe and its church and rectory on desolate and boggy ground amid the Essex marshes. Scarcely had he arrived and tipped the taxi-driver before doors started violently banging, altar flowers leapt from their vases and went flying down the nave, the credence bell clanged continually, and the Merryweather suitcase, dumped ready for clerical action in the vestry, jammed itself tight shut and refused to yield up the freshly laundered vestments within.

Worse was to come. Being graciously shown by the lady of the manor over the manor house, and lingering for a moment at a bedroom window to admire a fine piece of topiary work in the garden below, the Rev. Ernest, happily married and father of five, suddenly found himself being hotly embraced by a naked woman (the lady of the manor, I hasten to add, had gone on ahead, fully draped), with soft arms and softer breasts pressed to his canonicals. Thoroughly unnerved, and determined to be ready for anything. Mr Merryweather pedalled like a lamplighter into Chelmsford and equipped himself with an ornamental dagger, and then guess what! It was snatched from his belt by an unseen hand right in the middle of the collect for today. At all times the church hummed with activity. Repeatedly there was a whiff of out-of-season violets, mysterious women walked through the chancel walls, heavenly voices sang (uninvited, and I should hope so) plain-song, people were heard speaking in French (disgusting!), a woman's voice shouted 'You are a cruel man!', and in between whiles, crashes and bangs and shrieks rang out. One can only assume that congregations, unused to such exciting treats, arrived in coachloads from all over East Anglia, as they did for Matins with the Rector of Stiffkey, just off the early morning train from Soho.

We owe these details to Peter Moss who, darting inquiringly about the country, has been collecting the latest spectral news from all over everywhere. Ghosts tend in general to be female and fairly ancient, with scraped back white hair (buns are being worn again). Our highways and trunk roads are being increasingly haunted and I am able to give you, like the BBC's helpful morning announcements of black ice and burst water-mains and jack-knifed lorries, warnings of what to expect. Be particularly careful in the 'Gents' section of the Keele Service Area lavatory on the M6 (a Puritan, in full 17th century rig, standing motionless at the urinal). On the A3081 in Dorset, watch out for a Bronze Age horseman galloping along with very little road sense. The A427 provides a headless bicyclist on dark nights. There's a Victorian ghost child, sucking a toffee apple, on the A30 just this side of Bodmin, a balding bearded widower in green and pink pyjamas on the A279, and a wonky-looking phantom hitch-hiker (keen on lorry drivers) on the A38. To aid the imagination, Mr Moss's excellent book, *Ghosts Over Britain* (Elm Tree Books: £3.95), is strikingly illustrated by Angela Lewer, the surprising encounter in the Keele lavatory being especially vivid.

There has been, goodness me, such a lot going on even away from the roads. In W11, Phaïs Robert was subjected to foetid smells and rhythmic puffs of air. In Chorley hospital, despite an alert staff nurse ('Who has gone to the toilet?'), doors creaked inexplicably open and backless slippers shuffled to and fro. A startled lady called Gay Agnes of Coggeshall found her dead mother sensibly urging her to complete her household chores. A child in Bath was regularly visited by a chummy octogenarian wearing surgical boots. Near Durham, Ben Chicken found himself being stared at in bed by Mrs Chicken's defunct first husband looking reproachful. In Stow-on-the-Wold, large pools of water kept appearing on a polished floor (Pussy and Spot are both completely above suspicion).

In 1957, a Hampshire householder, finding his house haunted, applied to the local council for a reduction in rates. The reduction was granted. This seems to me easily the most improbable happening of all.

Getting To Know You

The lives of others are sometimes indeed a mystery wrapped in an enigma, or whatever that phrase is. Going with my parents to the 1924 Wembley Exhibition and calling at the Lost Property Office in search of an umbrella missing from a previous visit (my mother, intent on other matters, had left it in the Ladies), we were astonished to see, among the many mislaid objects on display, a full set of false teeth, promptly claimed by a fellow-inquirer who, to make quite sure they were his, instantly plunged them, careless of hygiene, between his gums and champed them up and down a few times, subsequently departing fully satisfied and, as with Miss Prism's handbag, delighted to have them so unexpectedly restored to him.

Now, in what possible circumstances could one, especially in the daytime, lose false teeth? Had he recklessly ventured on the Dodgems in the fun fair and had them jerked out of his mouth? Did they get embedded perhaps in a soggy Exhibition doughnut and had been absent-mindedly tossed into a refuse bin? Our brolly was rescued and later on we saw the teeth-owner again, happily flashing a big, gleaming smile at the British dairy-maids bravely churning their hearts out in the Butter Pavilion.

In the field of weird lives, wedded bliss particularly produces a poser or two. There is a theory that in a marriage, provided at least one of the two people concerned is absolutely determined to make it work, the partnership has a good chance of contented survival. Never having been called upon to sidle nervously up the aisle through pews boasting a proud display of unfortunate new hats and Sketchley-fresh garments, and squeak out an alarmed 'I do' at the altar steps, I am really unable to pronounce on such matters and all the happy couples that I know seem to be happy indeed. Who can tell whether both or either of them is struggling away to keep things maritally going behind the scenes, tactfully doing this, nobly refraining from doing that?

Some of the marriages culled at random from history's pages

do, though, provide rather thoughtful moments. Whatever can it have been like to have been Mrs Gladstone and on the receiving end of the Prime Minister, especially on those mornings (we know how philanthropically his evenings were spent) when William awoke feeling frisky and in the mood for tickles? Were her cries of 'Isn't it time you were getting down to the House, dear?' playfully smothered by the bolster? The over-crowded nurseries reveal only too clearly that few Victorian husbands took no for an answer. And, with one's thoughts running politically on, Mrs Baldwin's reactions on a similar occasion are well, if possibly apocryphally, known to us. But she, on the other hand, was surprisingly enough an ace cricketer and was doubtless accustomed to receiving those hard knocks at long leg that build character and help to fit one for life's battle. And one's sympathies fly across the years to another victim. It really can't have been much fun to have been Mrs Lincoln, before, that is to say, the little mishap.

The wedded conditions existing among a varied assortment of modern and outwardly ordinary couples are now placed before us in a volume sober in content but boldly entitled *Treat Yourself To Sex* ('A guide for good loving' encourage the fully qualified authors, Paul Brown and Carolyn Faulder, and Messrs Dent will hand over a copy for £4.95). Here, for all to see and brood on, are the married 'difficulties' experienced by a wide range of pairs chummily introduced to us as Wendy and Ray, Jane and Jack, Arthur (no relation) and Mavis, Sally and David, Peter and Fay, and Alec and Joan. You'll obviously want to know, delicately expressed, what the troubles were, and I'm sorry to say that it is generally agreed to have been principally the gentlemen who were at fault. Ray was off to dreamland the very moment his head touched the Dunlopillo, Jack had 'reverted to his bachelor habits' (unidentified), Arthur kept himself to himself and preferred to play a lone hand, David was reluctant to commit himself fully, while Peter's approach was over-hasty. Alec had merely lost his 'zip', a word which I place in inverted commas in case it should be supposed that Alec's bags were mechanically unsound and were flapping revealingly open. A sad record of failure, as you see, and perhaps echoed in many a home.

But stay! For those whose romances are now on the rusty side or which never in the first case amounted to anything very much, our kind authors suggest a stimulating five-day crash course for livening things up. Away at once with those inhibitions and get, as they say, stuck in. Day One finds you both peeling off every stitch of clothing and, in total silence, taking it in turns to examine yourselves intently in a full-length looking glass, peering now here, now there (a hand-mirror dexterously employed will assist you to take in parts not normally within visual reach). Day Two is the same as Day One but done in a flood of merry chatter. Jabber away like anything about your own body, and if you happen to feel like saying 'I do wish I had longer lobes', or whatever, just go right ahead and say it. Day Three finds us stripped off once more and at it again, only this time we 'pass remarks' about each other's bodies (although the authors urge us to be straightforward in criticism, I consider that, as a sample phrase, their suggestion of 'I find your behind is fat and lumpy' just a shade too personal). Day Four brings a change, welcome or not as the case may be. We place our heads in each other's laps and listen to whatever body noises happen to be going on at the time – thump thump, rumble rumble, gurgle gurgle. 'You may be dressed or not for this.' Thanks very much.

I am sorry to say that our final day, Day Five, presents a serious problem or two. Though the authors seek to hearten us by announcing that a certain type of male moth can smell the presence of his female counterpart at a distance of one and a half miles, some of us have really no wish at all to emulate this gift and smell anybody even at a distance of one and a half feet, yet this is exactly what we are now encouraged to do, moving in very much closer as the pace quickens. Worse is to come. 'Have a bath together', they advise. I feared as much. Who sits where, may I ask? Are we to be back to back or in a general jumble, legs and everything else in all directions? My bath at home accommodates me snugly enough but the insertion of another body would cause it instantly to overflow. Nor do I fancy sharing a sponge, let alone anything else.

However, for those who can manage these gymnastics, I have a helpful hint. At Christmas, a friend of mine was given some Perfumed Floating Candles. 'Use them in flower bowls and punch bowls' it said in the instructions on the box (hoping for a foreign market, the candles were also described as *Bougies Flottantes Parfumées*). Get some at once, for there was a further instruction, 'Float them in the bath for that special occasion'. If ever there was a special occasion, Day Five is it. Your doctor will advise you about the best treatment for burns in unusual places.

Cold Comfort Cottage

Our pleasing Devon village of Appleton has one priceless advantage. It is off the beaten track and on the way to nowhere. Not that the Teign Valley road, off which a narrower and less frequented way leads to us, exactly ranks as a beaten track, but it seems by comparison something of a smart highway, conducting southwards and westwards, as it does, eager motorists intent on shopping in Chudleigh (A.1. for veg.) or keen to press on to Newton Abbot and snap up a set of matching kebab skewers in its more sophisticated trading centre. Visitors come to Appleton neither for veg nor skewers. They come, if they come at all, to see friends. Any strange arrivals here arrive by mistake and have to be politely directed back whence they came. They go quietly and we return once more to rural peace.

We are situated in the Dartmoor National Park and will go to any lengths to preserve its charm and to prevent any vulgarisation or diminution of its beauties. Some years ago, a new and rather flashy inhabitant approached me and asked whether I would allow him to erect at the edge of my orchard a fish-and-chip boutique. The request was accompanied by knowing winks and nudges and hints that there would be 'something in it for you' (5 per cent of the profits was the extremely generous offer, and the run of my teeth on Mondays, vinegar ad lib). He has long since, a fish out of water, left the district. Appleton was plainly not for his kind. Smart-Alicks frying and selling fish and chipped potatoes are not at all in the spirit of the place.

The name Dartmoor means different things to different people. I have mentioned before our late village *blanchisseuse*, Mrs Hooper, who had never heard of George VI and whom, as I weekly deposited and collected my wash, I came to know quite well. To her, Dartmoor, on the picturesque fringes of which she had spent her life, meant solely the prison. It loomed large in her thinking and had become an obsession. Informed by gossipy neighbours that a prisoner had escaped and was on the run, she was invariably convinced that his plan was to make a bee-line for her, spreadeagle her on the bed and chop her head off. Dartmoor prison was a good 30 miles away but that distance would be a mere nothing to somebody with but one thought on his mind: 'Get Mrs Hooper!' To avert this little inconvenience, she used to leave her front door open for a night or two and put out a tasteful snack: beef sandwiches, jam tarts, a pick of cheese, light ale. The idea was to placate him and stop him mounting the stairs to do her in, and when I pointed out that such a substantial intake of vitamins, almost certainly on an empty stomach, would immediately supply the vigour so necessary for a really effective head-chopping, she was much flustered. Mrs Hooper lived on, every part of her intact, to the age of 86 and we miss her greatly.

Not every aspect of our life here below is, as we know, roses all the way and even Devon has two disadvantages. One of these occurs, alas, around 9 p.m. It is at about this hour, with dinner gently digesting within and the telly news just coming up, that we in the South West are treated to our daily sonic boom. Does it

. . . a tasteful snack to placate him

come from a French or British Concorde? How high is it flying? Is it coming or going? It matters little. It is a sound like no other – unnerving, unearthly and wholly detestable. It rattles roofs and shakes windows. Public opinion has already forced the authorities to reduce the aircraft's appalling din at take-off and landing, but there is nothing at all to be done about reducing a boom. It is a natural phenomenon invented by God, like earthquakes and tidal waves and other nastinesses, and it can't be tampered with. A boom is a boom, and poor old Devon and Cornwall, relatively sparsely populated areas and not greatly given to complaining, are evidently considered aurally expendable.

The other disadvantage is that we sometimes get weather that is obviously intended for others. Snow blizzards, with 'Scotland' written all over them, decide to drop in on us instead and take us all by surprise. I write in February and at a time when Appleton is cut off from the outside world and every single road in the county is closed. The sight of so much snow, deep and crisp and even, sends one's thoughts flying to Good King Wenceslas. I have often wondered whether the press of the day was friendly or hostile about that famous episode on the Feast of Stephen. Though outwardly a generous enough gesture, there was serious risk of hypothermia to the page, forced by the monarch to accompany him across the icy fields. There was another consideration, which the *Morning Post* of the day doubtless pointed out:

That the King's action during the recent cold snap was kindly meant, there can be no doubt. We merely question the wisdom of singling out one person alone for this sort of royal patronage. It smacks of favouritism and can only bring with it envy and bitterness.

The peasant honoured by the King, a Mr L. Goodchild, interviewed later in his cottage residence conveniently situated for supplies of both water and kindling wood, said 'You could have knocked us down with a feather, the old girl and me, when His Majesty waltzed in. Talk about surprise! We weren't half chuffed with the grub, and the wine went down a treat. At that moment, all we had in the house was a few rusks and a small tin of Slumberola (you just add milk).' Asked if he would again like to accept regal gifts of this nature, Mr Goodchild answered with a twinkle 'Too bloody true I would.'

It is understood that the royal park is now daily filled with peasants feverishly gathering winter fuel well within sight of the Palace windows.

Well, it has been Wenceslas Week here. At one point during the worst of the weather, our electricity failed and disappeared for 17 hours. In our remoteness, there is of course no gas supply and we are warmed and lit and cooked for electrically. Not all of

Appleton was thus deprived, I am glad to say, but just a small section in the centre of the village and consisting of the butcher-cum-grocer (anxious about his deep freeze), the village pub (prettily ablaze with candle-light and fully frequented), the sub-post-office-cum-stationer's (run by a truly saintly pair) and a small quantity of houses, dotted here and there and among them, you will be horrified to hear, 'Myrtlebank' itself. Why the South Western Electricity Board should single me out for this snub, I cannot imagine (bills paid on the dot, and the meter-reader refreshed with coffee if he calls during inclement weather. There's gratitude for you).

When, in the wintry gloom, it became clear which houses had power and which had not, little parties set out from the lighted houses and made their way through the snow to the houses in darkness, bringing with them comforts of every sort. At 'Myrtlebank' I welcomed, at intervals, a thermos of tea (Miss Entwhistle), a piping hot stew (Cousin Madge), mince pies (Mr and Mrs Harcourt) and a huge canister of soup, together with a slightly rickety camping stove on which to warm it (Canon Mountjoy). One was warmed by more than the soup. The human kindness available in our village is really very remarkable. But what, you ask, from the Bultitudes? Wings of chicken and all the etceteras? Silver buckets of caviare delivered by the chauffeur? Half a Stilton? Cobwebby bottles of port? The Bultitudes, first in line when it comes to generosity if irritating in almost every other way, are, need I say, abroad. At any moment, a shower of patronising and highly coloured post-cards of exotic foreign parts will descend on us ('Don't you *adore* Tangier?'). Had they been here, however, I can hardly think that the Electricity Board would have dared to insult *them*.

Oyez Oyez

Moving about London and the South of England as I do, now here, now there, I have come across two minor hazards of travel which, like VAT and hang-gliding and skateboards, are perilous modern inconveniences that are now plainly here to stay. The first hazard, the dazzling product of the finest minds in British Rail, is the installation, just about 50 years late, of public address systems in main line trains (I refuse to call them Inter-City. Where on earth do they think the lines ran before?). I am all in favour of these systems being present and ready for use in a crisis so that passengers may have up-to-the-minute news of breakdowns ('We have broken down') or of unexpected and surprise happenings ('We are now leaving the rails'), but of course the contraptions and their activating microphones have proved quite irresistible to members of the train's staff who perhaps see themselves as promising radio personalities, deafening us with chat laced, heaven help us all, with jokettas. Thus it is that disembodied voices loudly and constantly jerk one out of a pleasant doze by trying to drum up trade for the buffet's mouth-watering range of culinary delights, or by booming out gratuitous information of very minimal interest ('We have just passed Swindon'). How long before they take a leaf out of the notebook of British Airways? 'This is your engine-driver speaking. Welcome aboard! We shall be travelling at approximately 70 m.p.h. and at a height of about eight feet.'

I have a helpful suggestion to make. In the 1930s, and to help banish the tedium of rail travel, cinema carriages were available on some express trains, certainly on the LNER (the initials have a happy, nostalgic ring) and, for all I know, on other networks. One shilling and sixpence was the charge for an hour's showing of a selection of brief films of the sort that were then called, like some wistful paedophile's daydream, 'Shorts and Interest'. There was M. Mouse too. Well then, if these carriages still exist, let them be brought out, dusted down and filled, not with films

111

but with Art. British Rail has, as we know (and how wisely, time will tell), invested large sums of pension fund money in valuable pictures. Where, may one ask, are these treasures, purchased after all with cash extracted from you and me, housed? Why can't we see them? Get them on the move. A travelling picture gallery would make an agreeable addition to life on the 10.30 a.m. to Exeter. How much better, as we thunder through the numerous aesthetic calamities of Slough, to gaze instead at the superb brushwork of Constable, the extraordinary colours of Turner, the idyllic peace of a Corot landscape. The guard would, naturally, accord special favours to those passengers who have gone a bust and purchased first class tickets ('Would you care for a quick peep at my Pissarro?').

The second travel hazard involves motorised locomotion through the streets of London. Recently, after leaving the commodious NS offices and moving out into the yet wider world of High Holborn, I hailed a taxi and, stepping briskly in, answered the driver's now customary question of 'Where to, Squire?' with the words 'Paddington, please'. 'Ah,' he said as we drove off, 'I thought you looked a Paddington type.' Did you ever! Whatever can one make of it? So that you can judge for yourself, you'll need to know what I was wearing. My roomy, all-purpose 'Grenfell' macintosh ('By Appointment To The Queen' it says inside the collar), together with a not very nice tweed cap which serves to keep my hair in some sort of order. Marks & Spencer bags in a restful beige. Marks & Spencer shoes (if unknown to you, lash out on a pair. Half the price of anywhere else, and they last almost for ever). How on earth could my trim appearance suggest 'Paddington'? And if so, what rig would suggest 'Euston' or 'Victoria' or the dread confines of Liverpool Street, a station name so misleading for foreigners heading for Merseyside? I am reminded of *Punch* and of the drawing (was it by du Maurier?) of two very smart and worldly young ladies from W8 being observed by two old gentlemen. 'You can always tell a Kensington girl', runs the merriment underneath the picture, 'but you cannot tell her much.'

But being identified as a Paddington type was not the second hazard to which I referred. The hazard I meant is that, in my experience over the last five or so years, taxi-drivers, doing a lonely, isolated job and feeling out of things, now require to be solaced with conversation yelled above the traffic's din and through the partly open glass partition. Nine out of ten of them now want to chatter. And so my Paddington-spotter, after a preliminary flurry of courtesies ('Don't I know your voice?') launched away on a lengthy *cri de coeur* involving three female non-whites (as they were described) who had required him to wait for 20 minutes on some double yellow lines in the West Ham area while they visited a nearby launderama. A row about the fare had followed and the police had been summoned. During this somewhat biassed harangue and remembering our principles, I preserved a prim exterior and reminded him sharply, at its conclusion, that it takes all sorts to make a world. The vehicle noise in the Bayswater Road was such that it made this novel and interesting statement inaudible and I had to shriek it three times to get its message through. No offence taken. We parted on terms of the jolliest possible bonhomie ('Don't do anything I wouldn't do, Guv') at, indeed, Paddington, Gateway to the West.

How very odd names are. Why should 'Paddington', not so very long ago green fields and trees and cows munching, be so suitable a sound for a terminus? The British, both in fact and in fiction, are extremely good at names. What name could possibly have fitted the late, alas, owner of it more admirably than that of Richard Dimbleby? There was the solid promise of 'Richard' followed by the, somehow, pleasant roundness of 'Dimble', reminiscent as it is of 'dimple' and those dumpy Haig bottles but actually meaning dell or dingle, both entirely pleasurable words, with 'by' at the end to give it a little parting flourish. I doubt if any name in fiction is more exactly right in its appalling simplicity than that of Waugh's 'Captain Grimes' in *Decline and Fall*, 'Grimes' speaking for itself, with, in 'Captain', that reputable rank (though hardly so in this case) and that proof of respectability so desperately clung to by endless gallant, gas-damaged and underpaid prep-school masters of the 1920s.

There is not a name in Dickens that is not in every way perfection. Just think of them: Gamp, Squeers, Cheeryble, Pickwick, Fagin and Wilkins Micawber. Shakespeare, as one would expect, always gets names right, with one grave exception. Malvolio, Quince, Cleopatra – what could be better? Ditto Rosalind, Falstaff and Mercutio – who could imagine them being called anything else? The one that is so sadly at fault is the name allotted to Hamlet's fiancée, a hopeless enough girl at the best of times and hardly seen to advantage with straws in her hair and indecencies on her lips. But what chance did she ever have? No possible good is going to come to any character, either in fiction or in life itself, the first syllable of whose name produces the sound 'Oaf'. Even if, in your charity, you like to think of it as just being 'Oh', you are

113

then stuck with 'feel yer'. 'Oh feel yer' what, may I inquire, a dangerous question to which every ribald schoolboy, landed, so to speak, with *Hamlet,* knows a variety of answers.

Names Please

For reasons that are too multitudinous and self-evident to lay before you, the question of weight being by no means the least important, my name was not put forward for inclusion among those of the prospective scientific candidates due to be blasted off from earth in 1980 in a re-usable Space Shuttle and sent into orbit in order to work far away up there in a European Space-laboratory ('After you with that Bunsen'). It seems that almost anybody could apply for a seat on this unusual jaunt for which the exceptional athletic abilities required of those original moon-walkers are no longer needed and, as a result, over 2,000 people pressed forward, all eager for the treat. The passengers are in fact to be scientists rather than astronauts and the appalling cost is being met, without any reference to you and me of course, by the EEC and with Germany, I rejoice to say, being socked for a far higher proportion of the cash than poor old penniless England. The European applicants have now been short-listed and whittled down to four, only one of whom is going to join with other national representatives and attention focuses on the strongly fancied Dutch aspirant, aged 31, a recent snap showing him to be the possessor of a drooping handlebar moustache so lengthy and luxuriant that one fears it may get itself caught up in the delicate controls at lift-off and interfere with the sensitive mechanism. His name, I beg you to believe me, is Wubbo Ockels, so cries of 'Another sandwich, Wubbo?' and 'Good for you, Wubbo' may be heard echoing round the capsule.

Before I leave for the time being the, to me, fascinating subjects of names and America, do let me share with you excerpts from a book, *Remarkable Names of Real People*, kindly sent to me by an old friend now living in the US and formerly a distinguished editor of the *Times Literary Supplement*. It is a compilation by gifted John Train of what turn out to be mainly American names, a real connoisseur's collection of genuine oddities (invented names are no fun at all) put together with help of an international network of assiduous correspondents. A preface by none other than S. J. Perelman is, as they say in the textile trade, a guarantee of quality. The enterprising publisher is Clarkson N. Potter of New York and this splendid volume has been published over here by the Harvester Press Ltd.

A lady from Lakeland, Florida, anxiously wondering whether she had the world's funniest name, which happened to be Mrs Verbal Funderburk, wrote to Mr Train to inquire and found that she was really pretty much of an also-ran, Mr Train easily calming her with a reference to two art school students from Minneapolis who were called Tunis Wind and Sharon Willfahrt, both of them classmates of Cinderella Hardcock, the history of art being safe in the hands of a New York art historian named Violet Organ. And Mrs Funderburk was lucky in another way. We all know the American custom by which women retain their own surname after marriage, merely tacking on to it that of their spouse. Picture then the plight of a Miss Belcher who married a Mr Wack. On Mr Wack's decease, she promptly married, evidently liking the product, his brother and thus wound up facing the world as Mrs Belcher Wack Wack.

It is the first impact of an unusual name that is so potent: a number of repetitions and then its fresh charm is gone and, moreover, one can get accustomed to anything. For example, I was at school with a boy called Boddham-Whetham, a name which, after we had merrily mispronounced it for a week, became to us as ordinary as Henderson. The book we are discussing understandably quotes our own British admiral, Sir Cloudsley Shovel, but that is a name as familiar and unremarkable to us as his skilful feat of running the entire fleet full tilt into the rocky and unyielding Scilly Isles, drowning whole shiploads of sailors and getting himself buried in Westminster Abbey as a reward. However, Mr Train swiftly makes up for this non-surprise by reminding us that the officer commanding the Guantanamo Naval Base was a Captain Bigge Boozer. Again, our compiler finds pleasure in Miss Horsey de Horsey, though of course we have known for years that she was a close friend in the Crimea of that frightful Lord 'Half a League' Cardigan.

But it is the US that scoops the prize and delightful novelties can always be expected from a nation which can take in its stride such Christian names as Chlorine, Twitty, La Urine, Zippa, Coita, Arson, Dewdrop, La Morte, Dinette, Bugger, Cad and Constipation, and on and into the even wider world of memorable surnames in which America never lets us down — Aphrodite

Chuckass, Sexious Boonjug, Zita Apathy, Heidi Yum-Yum Gluck and Sistine Madonna McClung. But though the New World may excel, other countries occasionally ring the bell. When in the 1930s a prominent White Russian leader was seized by OGPU agents in the streets of Paris and spirited away, disguised as merchandise, on to a Russian ship, the lynx-eyed French *commissaire de police* in charge of the case was Charles Adolphe Faux-Pas Bidet. To distract his mind from this dramatic and puzzling affair, one can only hope that in his leisure moments he enjoyed a little light literature, possibly the works of an authoress now, alas, but seldom read, Madame Fouqueau de Pussy.

In the 1920s, various English wags, discovering in the telephone directory the name of a Mrs Trampleasure, used to ring her cheekily up to ask whether she had that day had her pennyworth. A similar fate befell a Hollywood actress called Gisella Werberserch-Piffel who repeatedly received telephone calls asking whether she was by any chance the Gisella Werberserch-Piffel whom the caller had met in, say, Monte Carlo. On receiving a cold denial, the caller's answer was invariably 'Ah, then that must have been *another* Gisella Werberserch-Piffel.' Other names lay themselves open to endless impertinences – the Jamaica attorneys Lawless & Lynch, a Louisiana hospital official called

His name is Wubbo Ockels

Luscious Pea, a singing teacher from British Columbia (Mrs Screech) and, by contrast, an editor of the *Christian Science Monitor* (Silence Bellows), together with the Norfolk plumbing firm of Plummer & Leek and a Houston social leader called Ima Hogg.

Almost my favourite name belongs to yet another resident of New York City, Bambina Broccoli. I see her as very *petite* and animated and possibly a neighbour of little Mrs Tiney Sprinkle, about whose life one longs to know more. Then I have room and to spare in my heart for Fanny Fangboner (a nurse from Ohio), a native of Maryland (Noble Teat), an Italian contractor called O. Hell, an Australian undergraduate (Grecian T. Snooze), a gentleman named, and very inappropriately I feel sure, Gaston J. Feeblebunny, and when I die, I wish my remains to be attended to by the Quick-Park Funeral Home of Sandusky, proprietor Goody P. Creep, though I had some little difficulty in deciding between him and a Houston undertaker called Groaner Digger.

Wider Still and Wider

Among life's inconveniences and difficulties, which, for insomniacs in the still watches of the wakeful early mornings, sometimes magnify themselves into a positive cornucopia of nastinesses emptied on to their heads and all of which nastinesses I personally choose to lay at the door of the Supreme Architect (well, He could have prevented them, could He not, if He had wished to?), the problems raised by teeth must rank pretty high. Teeth are nothing but a nuisance from the cradle, where we painfully cut them, to the grave, by which time most of them have equally painfully gone, replaced by dazzling falsities nestling in bright pink gums and clicking their way noisily through the Krunchysnaps and the Jiffyburgers and the creamy Hastimash ('every nourishing globule fashioned from genuine potato').

I have so far been able to avoid a clanking mouthful of manufactured articles, settling instead for the dwindling imperfections supplied to me long ago by Dame Nature, one of which, rather prominently placed, got badly chipped at cricket, a game I played at school because it was compulsory to do so and you were beaten if you didn't. Our wicket-keeper had one day gone down, as we used to phrase it, with pink eye and I volunteered to take his place, not at all minding being rather more in the public eye and assuming that the activities necessary so near the wicket would be more interesting than those required of me at long-stop, a position on the field where one could quite easily have died without being much noticed ('Why is that boy lying down?'). Anxious to display keenness (sucking up to some senior, I don't doubt), I stood, unfortunately, much too close to the stumps and an odious opposing player struck me full in the mouth with his bat. Apologies followed but the conventions of the day made it impossible for me either to blub or, before the game was over, to leave the field for repairs by Matron. My attacker went on to do extremely well in the higher ranks of the civil service. Draw your own conclusions.

Circumstances forced me some ten years ago to change dentists, a happening that bothers the stoutest hearts. I used to go, rather swankily for me, to Harley Street and to the world's best and nicest (and, as it happens, cheapest) dentist. On his sad retirement, the first bill presented to me by his young replacement was so horrifyingly high that I took fright, abandoned the W1 area and daringly placed myself in the hands of the National Health, since when, coupled with efficiency and speed, all has been strangeness and novelty and fascination.

In Harley Street, animated conversation had been *de rigueur,* it being not too easy at times to answer questions with one's mouth chock-a-block with assorted contraptions ('What do you think of Mr Heath?'). Accustomed to this polite exchange of views on politics and the world in general, I attempted chatty overtures of a social nature with my first National Health representative ('Where are you spending your hols?') but they were received in a reproving silence and, to shut me firmly up, he switched on some music, of a sort. The music-dispensing machine was, or so I understood him to say but in my humiliation I may have got it all wrong, a new invention and its sound, unheard by the outside world, passed up the drill and on to my teeth and thence, via various bones inside my head, to my drums. My question as to why it couldn't take the more direct route through the open air went chillily unanswered: he was a little deaf, perhaps, a handy defect for a dentist to possess (all groans and screams inaudible). When the drilling began, I listened attentively and with great difficulty through the whirring noises and the accompanying splashy jets of water, and I could just dimly hear something that, on a good day so to speak and with the wind in the right quarter, could well have been a tuneful selection from *The Desert Song.* Still, I was getting it for free, or nearly so, and I appreciatively and tactfully hummed along for a bar or two. When I first used to leave this dentist's room, he seemed always to hiss something very crossly at me and then slam the door behind me. I had, as is my way, been all courtesy with him, so wherefore such huffiness? Subsequent visits, however revealed that the hissing and slamming came from one of those door-shutting applicances. Offputting, all the same.

Passed on, understandably, from one operator to another, I am now in the hands of a nice lady dentist, Miss D, splendidly capable and she cannot be a day over 25. With her, music by-passes my molars and comes straight and loudly into the ear from a transistor permanently tuned to the wild morning jollinesses of

Radio 2. And under her attentions and guidance. I entered an entirely new dental world. Gone is the frightening panoply of alarming instruments poised at the ready above one's face and at which one gazed horror-struck, with among them something round and bomb-like and reminiscent of an old-fashioned *machine infernale* destined for a crowned head but which was in reality, I think, merely a counterweight to the cumbersome drill and its attendant propulsive cords. Vanished are the basin, the whirling water, the rinse-please tumbler filled with a reddish prophylactic. Absent is the chair which, pedalled by the dentist, went up and down together with its adjustable head-rest ('There! Is that quite comfortable?'). Instead, in a room at first glance as bare as one recently visited by hard-hearted bailiffs, I am requested to lie out flat on a sort of extra large oil-clothed surf board and Miss D, sinking down on to a stool, produces with a conjuror's flourish her dental instruments, invisible and therefore unworrying, from somewhere behind me. And away we go.

We are not alone. Seated within six inches of my head is another lady, equally young. A student? An assistant? A friend who has just dropped by and has half an hour to kill before her bus? This one also peers, two heads being better than one I suppose, into my cavities and occasionally lends a hand with a deft squirt of water or a puff of cold air (often so much more painful than the drill). One has therefore to be on the alert for attentions from two quarters. Conversation hardly exists and is strictly limited to the work in hand. In the prone position, swallowing tends to be a bit difficult and convulsive but otherwise all is quickness and efficiency. When all that can be done for my teeth has been done and I have struggled upright, telling myself that I don't feel rather dizzy, Miss D informs me that she will later on wish me to see 'our hygienist'. She, it appears, is booked solid for five weeks and is plainly all the rage. Fresh excitements ahead! I ask what her function is. 'She will scale you and polish you and tell you how to brush your teeth.' At last, at last; and at the age of 67, the information comes not one moment too soon.

I am lucky in that I have never needed to have any real fear of dentists. Many years ago, while living in Northamptonshire, I used to visit in Wellingborough a wonderfully competent and agreeable Scottish dentist called Shearer. It was nothing but a pleasure to go and see him. Examining my teeth in the early days, he was kind enough to pay a polite tribute ('Beautiful work!') to previous tillers in this field. After an extraction, you were encouraged to lie down for a while in a rest room before going home, and tea and biscuits were brought, a prudent measure unavailable on the NHS. If a tooth's future was doubtful, he used to mutter: 'We must put up a wee prayer for this fellow.' His patients were not referred to as such by him. We were not patients but 'mouths'. Conversation flowed. 'One of our most interesting mouths has just returned from France . . .' 'I was playing golf the other day with one of our mouths . . .' He told me that he found faces very hard to remember. Meeting in the street somebody vaguely familiar and wishing to place him, he used to ask him to say 'Ah'. When, a little baffled, the unknown obligingly opened his mouth and did so, Mr Shearer would swiftly peer inside and recollect the name in a trice. He has, I am afraid, long since been dead. If there are teeth in heaven, and how else may I ask are we going to eat *foie gras* to the sound of trumpets, I shall make a bee line for him.

He will be, I am afraid, much in demand. I can't think that Mozart could ever have afforded very much in the way of elaborate dental treatment. We know a bit about Elizabeth I's fangs, but what of Goethe's canines? History is woefully silent on the subject of Bacon's gums. But whatever their little troubles, Mr Shearer will be finding them all to be 'fascinating mouths' and I look forward to a tremendous chin-wag.

Lead with the Chin

As loyal readers of this column will recall, perhaps all too clearly, I do from time to time gaze back down life's blossom and boulder-strewn pathway and cull here and there from among my many and varied nuggets of experience a useful hint or two which I freely pass on to others. Invited recently by the BBC to provide a thoughtful minichat of 3½ minutes' duration for broadcasting during Easter Week on Woman's Hour, the unusually wide response that my talk provoked (letters from all over, and a 1lb box of dairy-milk chocs from a charmingly over-excited listener in Goole), encourages me to share its valuable lesson with you in more permanent form here. I had been asked to trot out some little saying or other that I had found helpful down the years and I provided one from, of all unsuitable areas for me, the world of fisticuffs. In addition to playing cricket and football, we were at my prep school all forced to 'do' boxing. Boxing was manly and the authorites had confidence that the noble art would succeed in making men of us, or something. And so, every Thursday afternoon at 2 p.m. I climbed, aged nine, into a boxing-ring and stood there facing a boy invariably a foot taller and two stones heavier and wearing an expression of a repulsively belligerent nature. A gong sounded and we boxed, by which I mean I just stood there patiently while he hit me. My nose bled, my eyes closed and after some time there came the moment when the referee shouted the joyous word STOP.

At first when this happened, I assumed it meant that the little contest was at an end and I looked forward to climbing out of the ring, removing my gloves and getting on with chapter XV of Bulldog Drummond's adventures in *The Black Gang* (poor Phyllis Benton in some frightful pickle or other – it was no joke being Mrs Drummond – and getting gassed outside the Ritz down a taxi's speaking-tube). But not at all. The hiatus merely meant that the referee wished to ascertain whether I was still alive and breathing and, on finding that I was, he shouted the dread words

Boxing was manly

BOX ON and I started to be hit all over again. 'Box on' is, I suppose, a goodish motto for coping with life's buffets and I do not regret the maulings.

At my age, I make no apologies for harking back, and indeed there is not much of interest to hark forward to, and so, keen as I am on entertainment in general and the stage in particular, let me place before you a theatrical quiz, to which a recent sad event gives point. I do realise that by plunging nostalgically into the happy London past when Shaftesbury Avenue was crammed at 2.15, not with camera-slung foreigners asking to be directed to Kew but with tidily-dressed British persons on their way to matinees, and theatre dressing-rooms were filled with actresses striving to make themselves even lovelier and giving their dressers what for ('Quick, Estelle, another Kirbygrip!'), I risk upsetting yet again that public-spirited correspondent who takes me to task about my 1920s theatre-going. Never mind. The quiz relates to a time about ten years before this, with Gertie Millar still an enchanting memory as *Our Miss Gibbs* and Leslie Henson splitting everybody's sides in *To-night's The Night*. Ready? Who was the Cambridge graduate who leapt (it was then a rather rare occurrence) straight from the university onto the professional musical comedy stage and into a gigantic floperoo called *The Light Blues*, which had in it a number which went

I'm Cuthbert the Coconut,
The smartest on the tree,
And any girl who isn't shy
Can try a shy at me.

Who (same man) then married one of the show's leading ladies, a performer of stunning talent then playing an *ingénue* called Popsy Velour, and lived happily ever after? Who, and this will give it away, had one of the longest chins in the business?

I have neither the intention nor the right to set myself up as the official NS stage obituarist but when less than justice has been done elsewhere, however unintentionally, to a widely admired and well liked actor who pleased the public for over 60 years, I turn into 'Disgusted, Devon' and can no longer refrain, as we disgruntled letterwriters phrase it, from taking up my pen. Not that anybody was actually disagreeable about Jack Hulbert, and indeed it would have been quite impossible to be so, but just a rather tedious string of titles of the musicals and films in which he appeared, which is what most newspapers tamely settled for, gives us and posterity no idea of his important place in the theatrical musical panorama.

There had been lean and lanky and loose-limbed leading men before him, Joseph Coyne and George Grossmith among them, and there was a real fizzer yet to come (Jack Buchanan), but there was nobody who looked, in splendidly cut pin-stripe suits, more as though, on his way on some sunny day to shop in Bond Street, he had stumbled by mistake through the stage door and was now strolling, with sleek fair hair and blue eyes and an apologetic chuckle, out in front of an audience, prepared to dance a little, sing (rather nasally) a little, and act not very much. He seemed to be the apogee of nonchalance, professionally one of the hardest effects to achieve, and he could charm the birds from the trees. If I make so bold as to say that he looked like, which indeed he was, a gentleman, I suppose that in, and what dreary words they are, 'the climate of today' I shall be subjected to derision. Well, I can take it.

In the dear dead days before revues decided to be rude and

disagreeable and generally beastly about everybody and every-thing (I think they call it satirical) and abandoned even the faintest attempt to make themselves visually agreeable (can any-thing be uglier than those banks of exposed spotlights, flagrantly flaunted?), Jack Hulbert produced, concurrently with Cochran and Charlot, a glittering fistful of such entertainments with, in his case and as their particular star, Cicely Courtneidge (for that simpering *ingénue* of 1915 in a pink silk dress with panniers and a Dolly Varden hat, archly singing a song called 'Don't you go a-counting of your chickens', was none other than she, as though you hadn't guessed.) There had been revues before but they had largely been friendly and rather casual affairs relying mainly on a collection of big names (*The Co-Optimists* had at least eight, ditto Pelissier's entrancing *Follies*) who sometimes struggled, as Noël Coward remembered, with indifferent lyrics:

Isn't it awfully jolly,
Doing a little revue!
Never could be a more happy idea,
It's nobby and nutty and new!

In them, beautiful show girls, often seeming only half awake, draped themselves in unoccupied corners of the stage and would have frowned disdainfully at any director who requested them to dance or, even, to move at all. The Hulberts changed all that. Nothing was left to chance. They hoarded fine material. All was speed and attack. The choruses were drilled like guardsmen. Revues became precision instruments, amalgams of wit and melody and talent and beauty and hilarity and charm and, what the theatre is really *for*, straight enjoyment and we should, in grateful memory, bow to one of their prime creators.

On We Go Again

I recently drew attention to some of the oddities of the Twenties and the peculiarities and weaknesses and purposeless lives of the Thirties that led foreigners, Hitler and Ambassador Kennedy among them, to consider us easy meat for conquerors. And then suddenly, in 1940, all became purposeful and the fun was finished. A few quaintnesses, it is true, continued (in the third year of the conflict, Lord Alvingham, former MP for South Dorset, complained in *The Times* that his title had been omitted from his ration book) but by and large frivolous behaviour was temporarily shelved. Even the most modest among us must agree that our war record at least stands up to examination. It may, of course, be argued that a nation fighting for its life needs to do just that but this was hardly so with our nearest neighbours across the Channel who initially, and here one lapses into half-forgotten army phrases, put up a markedly wet performance, a performance comfortably beaten by the Italians, for whose years of feeble, craven conduct and treachery they should be blushing to this day (so difficult to tell whether those dusky-complexioned Southerners are still suffused with shame or not. It's just a guess but I would think probably not).

In 1945 and with the European hostilities safely over, Churchill, setting off on an election tour, is reported to have said wistfully to Lord Moran, 'I feel lonely without a war'. War of a different sort was upon him but what he really meant, I suppose, was that he felt aimless and it was this that, after the first and quickly exhausted elation and relief were over, was indeed the general feeling. And in this limp deflation period, oddities started cropping up all over again. The source of the, to me, fascinating facts of last week and this is a book called *Gossip, 1920–1979* (Hamish Hamilton, £10.00, handsomely produced and splendidly illustrated) in which Andrew Barrow, born in the very year of Churchill's loneliness and diligently digging in such branpies as the *Tatler*, newspaper gossip columns, diary pages, autobiographies, *The Times* Court Circular and so on, has come up with an extraordinary number of items that now seem, as before, barely credible.

On his last day on earth, the King shot nine hares and one pigeon. Everybody got tremendously cross about Picasso and Matisse ('They verge upon the obscene'). Chips Channon, at an upper-crust reception at the Argentine Embassy, was heard to say excitedly 'This is what we have been fighting for'. Hermione Baddeley opened a mussel bar near Victoria Station. The 'evening-dress only' rule returned to the Savoy Grill. Lack of an export licence prevented Nubar Gulbenkian from bringing a Portuguese rose-velvet smoking jacket into England. The Duke of Windsor announced that he would write his memoirs ('I have lots of material'). Prince Philip of Greece applied, at a cost of £10 2s 6d, for British nationality. The Marquess of Salisbury was found to be doing his own washing up (demoted from washing to drying because of breaking too much china) and Mrs Wilson turned her sheets sides to middle. When one of the stately Buccleuch homes was re-opened, the Duke found 14 small Van Dycks hanging in a lavatory. Earl Spencer, keen on making more space, dug up several dead ancestors who had been quietly resting near Daventry and had them cremated ('I do not wish to discuss it'). Meanwhile, Lady Cunard's ashes were scattered in Grosvenor Square, despite the increasing smartness of Belgravia as a place of abode. The Duke of Bedford public-spiritedly sold a bison weighing over 400lbs to a London restaurant.

At the Grosvenor House débutantes ball, an attempt was made to blow up the ceremonial cake. The Dockers (by which we mean Sir Bernard and Lady) were found living on grapefruit at a Tring health-centre ('It is an internal spring-clean') before leaving in a new cream-and-gold Daimler upholstered in zebra ('Mink is too hot to sit on'). One of the Royal corgis bit a Buckingham Palace sentry. Stately homes had everywhere been thrown open and while the millionth visitor to Blenheim got a valuable eighteenth-century silver salver engraved with the family crest, the millionth one at Arundel got a box of chocs, the Blenheim gift being particularly generous after the Duke of Marlborough had complained that 'people will shuffle and wear out my carpets'.

Nowhere to be found were the high spirits of the twenties. The strict rationing, worse than in some wartime years and which continued, in one form or another, until 1954, simply did not produce the energy for high spirits and food was very much on everybody's minds, a subject of endless interest. Some did rather better than others. Lady Caroline Thynne, daughter of the Marquess of Bath, was 'launched' at a dance (crabs, lobster, champagne), while the American *bonne vivante* and party-giver, Elsa Maxwell, found herself dining at the House of Commons with Hartley Shawcross and gazing bemusedly at a whale steak. A waiters' strike at the Savoy forced patrons to manage as best they could with cold goose, chicken and salad, while Queen Mary, celebrating her eighty-first birthday, could only run to 'a small iced cake'. There was an Annigoni dinner at Prunier's (lobster, and quite enough some might think) while elsewhere the Royal Academicians were tucking into fish patties, roast beef and Stilton. General Eisenhower dined in Downing Street (Pudding Diplomatique) while the Douglas Fairbanks Jrs were dishing out, in classier SW10, cold salmon and curried chicken.

The better hotels seemed to manage fairly well. Lady Docker in flame-pleated tulle, was able, with the help of Claridges, to provide 200 chums with soles in champagne, while Churchill, celebrating a political swing to the right, lunched 'quietly' at the Savoy on dressed crab, Irish Stew, ice-cream and Stilton. Macmillan became Prime Minister (oysters and steak at the Turf Club), Princess Margaret lunched in Trinity College, Cambridge (tournedos, cauliflower Béarnaise and mash), and Princess Anne was hostess at tea at Buckingham Palace to fellow members of her Brownie pack (marzipan toadstools).

It was abroad, however, that the richest nutritional pickings were to be, for some, found. Churchill, dining in Morocco with the Pasha of Marrakesh, filled up empty corners with whole roast sheep and chickens stuffed with almonds and honey. Moving on to Villefranche, there was saddle of lamb and provençal herbs. At Chantilly, the Duff Coopers provided curry, hard-boiled eggs and rice, while anybody lucky enough to be approaching England in the Queen Elizabeth lunched on oysters, entrecôte steaks, asparagus in Hollandaise sauce and meringues. The young Lord Furness whizzed over to Paris with a party of friends and, for dinner, Maxim's produced caviar, foie gras, oysters, truffles and steaks. 'It's just like old times' said Albert, the head waiter. Yes indeed. Sometimes, then and now, I really rather wonder why we bothered to win at all.

Mr Barrow clangs the facts relentlessly out and with (he is, as we remember, only 33) only an occasional and fully justified show of contempt for some of those who took part in these strange gyrations. Perhaps his own middle and later years may, for one never knows, read as oddly. One improving word, however. A book composed entirely of facts really must get those facts right. An extraordinary inaccuracy proclaims that Miss, now Dame, Cicely Courtneidge, our beloved and longest-running comedienne (she kicked off professionally in 1909) appeared with Ivor Novello in his musical, *King's Rhapsody*. Whatever as, for heaven's sake? As a tweedy Queen Mother in a Henry Heath hat and gaiters and doing a funny dance with a sceptre? But what fun if she had!

Stars in My Eyes

Despite the helpful facilities once offered to us Senior Citizens by some moviehouse managers (reduction of 10p if seated in the front row by 2 p.m.), I have seldom in recent years undertaken a cinema outing, preferring to remain at home and revel in many stills from my happy filmic past thrown on the mind's eye by memory's projector. I go back really quite a long way. My cinema visits began in the first world war when, in addition to the main treat, short comedies such as *Put Pa Among the Girls, He Did Not Know He Was a Monk* and *Oh! That Terrible Odour* were all the rage. A No 9 bus whisked my mother and me from Gaumontless Barnes over the suspension bridge to exotic Hammersmith and Mary Pickford, 'The World's Sweetheart', who appeared, now as an Italian lighthouse keeper betrayed by a German spy, now as a plucky southern orphan rescuing children from an alligator-infested swamp dotted, for good measure, with quick-sand. Every now and then, she used to skip girlishly behind bushes and then peep winningly out. When people in films behaved badly, the audience hissed. When people behaved well, they applauded. Nowadays of course they don't do either, further sad evidence of the country's apathy. If at *A Bridge Too Far* I had loudly clapped one of the many valorous deeds, I should doubtless have been turned out for creating a disturbance and ('We know your sort') insulting behaviour.

My mother never dreamt of vetting our films. We just went along and took whatever chanced to be on offer and thus it was that I was able to feast my eyes on the ample charms of the original vamp, Theda Bara in *A Fool There Was,* an enormous lady with George Robey eyebrows and far more black hair than seemed strictly necessary and who, when not playing havoc with male hearts, tended to sit slumped in a corner, looking sulky and smouldering. I thought her the funniest object that I had yet seen and let out a series of delighted shrieks. Prior to films, Theda Bara had had stage experience, unwisely calling herself Theodosia de

Coppett, and the studio publicity department defiantly announced her as having been born in the very shadow of the Sphinx, love-child of a French artist and his Arab mistress. She was no such thing but the offspring of respectable Mr and Mrs Goodman of Cincinnati.

Other and more recent memories come flooding back – *Man of Aran* in which the main stars seemed to be, if memory serves, large lumps of seaweed and some wizened potatoes struggling to

Grapes invariably signalled hot stuff

survive on a rocky shore that was rather short on soil. Then there was Queen Victoria being shown, only a few years ago, a submarine ('Very unsportsman-like. What will these scientists think of next?'), charming Ann Todd providing extra Christmas gaiety with a number called 'Santa sent me you', and dear Merle Oberon, not very convincingly got up as George Sand, turning testily on the chunky Chopin of Cornel Wilde, banging away for dear life at the Bechstein, with 'discontinue that so-called Polonaise jumble you have been playing for days.'

An unenviable task that came my way as a schoolmaster and which I nobly shouldered for some twenty years was the choosing of the films that were, every three weeks or so, shown to the entire school and staff in the school hall. This little chore was mine because, among other eccentricities, I was supposed to be faintly in touch with the world of entertainment, and it was unenviable because of the extreme difficulty of pleasing such a widely assorted audience. Short of providing a celluloid excitement unavailable at the time but which would have silenced criticism, namely a jocular Movietone Newsreel of the Second Coming ('The four-engined Handley Page circles and – oops! – touches down rather heavily at Croydon and there at the cabin window, blinking a little in the unfamiliar flashlights, sits . . .'), I could only aim at delighting an average member of the audience.

But where did this average lie? Oundle comprised 700 schoolboys with ages stretching from 10 to 18, their tastes ranging from Buster Keaton to sophisticated Claudette Colbert in roguish mood. Then there were 12 matrons (I here use the word in its 'care of the sick' sense), resplendent in evening togs and still only vaguely redolent of arnica and iodine and longing to be taken out of themselves by a peep at Ronald Colman's moustache or Johnny Weissmuller's remarkably generous bulges. There were several other matrons (and here I use the word in its 'elderly lady of staid and sober habits' sense), married to members of the teaching staff and prepared to be sniffy about almost anything that wasn't Anna Neagle. There were, goodness me, the staff themselves, a collection of clever oddities bristling with prejudices and ready, like judges, to display ignorance ('Who is this Greta Garbo?') of everyday matters.

Luckily, when my selection stint began in 1933, the 'talkies' were well established and Hollywood was carefully minding its morals, for I recall, as a schoolboy, one or two unfortunate film choices. One of these was the famous *Intolerance*, D. W. Griffith's brilliant panorama of man's inhumanity to man. The film ran for

3½ hours, so we had two hours of inhumanity, scurried home for a quick supper (cauliflower cheese, as like as not) and then hurried back to find them being inhumane to each other all over again. At some point and in, I suppose, the ancient Babylon section, there was an ancient Babylon orgy.

In silent films they always indicated that an orgy was in the offing by producing bunches of luscious grapes, with people lying down sideways to eat them. Grapes invariably signalled hot stuff. Inflamed with Vitamin C taken horizontally, anything might happen. It was long before the days when Hollywood became prissily purity-conscious and so there were proud ancient Babylonian beauties gobbling grapes like mad and striking provocative poses whichever way you looked. Boys seated near the screen could have leant forward and positively touched partially draped bosoms. The staff looked gloomy for days on end and it was feared that the school maids would now be even more at risk than usual.

On another occasion, the modern language and music staffs, hot for culture, combined to press for the showing of a German silent film of *Der Ring des Nibelungen* with English sub-titles to help explain the unfolding action ('Brünnhilde in Siegfried's arms is all woman'). To add to the excitement, Wagnerian themes galore were thundered out on the school organ. All went well until the moment when Siegfried, a blond beast quite spent after making swords and cleaving anvils and leaping about after his bride-to-be, decided to take a refreshing dip in a studio pool conveniently to hand. Swiftly discarding various items of equipment – belt, mangy furs, those frightful crossgarterings – and kicking off his sandals, he peeled off his tunic and treated us, not to a full frontal, but to a full rearview of a vast German bottom wobbling its way beneath the healing waters. At this point, the music having momentarily stopped, I and certain other members of the house I was in, feeling that something was needed, applauded. Fatal mistake, as it turned out, and we got a fearful wigging from the housemaster whom I have mentioned ('You have blackened our face in public'). So much for trying to help things along.

But This is Monstrous!

Soft-hearted as I am (a further sign, if any was required, of my general feebleness and ineptitude), I have always been distressed in life by any kindness planned by one person for another and intended as a pleasant surprise or a treat or an unexpected gift and which has then chosen to 'go wrong' and has produced nothing but glum faces and grumpy expressions. When I was seven, an adopted aunt, a species that was often more on the ball than the real ones, came to tea, bearing with her a gift snapped up in W. H. Smith. It was a copy of the latest yarn, as we called them, by Captain (later Major) Charles Gilson. The first world war was drawing to a close and the book was called *Submarine U93*, a thrilling adventure story of warfare above and beneath the waves. She handed it over, beaming, and then stood back, expectant of smiles. But I already possessed the book and knew it nearly by heart. The disappointment was too great to be borne and I burst, natch, into floods. So much for *that* jolly little surprise. It was always even more distressing when a planned treat had gone wrong while heading in one's own direction.

My Cousin Madge relates that on her eighth birthday in 1899, she was allowed to celebrate the day by choosing three unaccustomed treats. Her birthday fell that year on a Sunday and so naturally the first treat of her choice was not to have to go to church. Doubtless this produced gasps of dismay and disapproving looks but a promise was a promise. Church-going was, in her case, an especially trying ordeal as her mother played the harmonium for the services and Madge, seated in the front pew and much *en évidence*, had to preserve a dignified appearance through various discords and imperfect harmonies and the moments when her mother, exhausted with pedalling, supplied the harmonium with insufficient wind and it squeaked into silence.

The second treat that she selected from the exciting possibilities available was to eat an entire tin of condensed milk. And the third was to ride up and down all morning on a donkey. The condensed milk was produced, a donkey was borrowed from a farm a mile away, and Madge's mother set out for church, with a reproachful glance, I expect. Madge then climbed an apple tree, ate all the condensed milk and was immediately sick. She then hoisted herself onto the donkey, but, finding perambulation in the drive somewhat dull and unenterprising, opened the gate and urged her mount to head for the open road. But the donkey, realising that nothing now lay between it and home, instantly threw Madge into a thick thorn hedge, tearing her dress, and legged it for the farm. So much for *those* little treats.

A really impressive instance of a happy surprise turning into a series of total disasters was supplied by a married couple, friends of friends, who lived abroad in a country district. They had had a small tiff and the husband decided to go to the neighbouring town to purchase a kiss-and-make-up present for his loved one. Perhaps, while deciding what to buy, he had a glass of wine, a prudent course of action. Perhaps the choice seemed especially difficult and he had two or three prudent glasses for in the end what he actually bought for her was a parrot in a cage. He then set out for home. Arriving within sight of the house, he opened the cage door for a friendly peep at polly, and the parrot, no fool, at once flew out and up into the topmost branches of a high tree. The husband climbed after it and, half way up, slipped and fell heavily to the ground, breaking a leg. His shriek of agony so startled the parrot that it left its tree-top perch and flew further off onto a tall pole with thick wires attached to it (parrots can talk but not read and the words DANGER DE MORT meant nothing to it). There it alighted, immediately burst into flames and fell, a ball of fire, into a field of ripe corn, setting it ablaze from end to end. And so the wronged wife, alerted by the din and emerging hurriedly from the house, found herself with an empty parrot cage, a badly damaged husband and, subsequently, an enormous bill from the furious farmer for his badly damaged corn. So much for *that* little kiss-and-make-up present.

And so it was that when a very charming and then Highgate-based actress of my happy acquaintance invited me to lunch, and added 'I've got a little surprise for you,' I had an anxious moment. She could hardly at this late stage be going to give me *Submarine U93*. Were there donkeys or parrots or, indeed, condensed milk in Highgate? Time would tell. On the morning of the beano she rang, thoughtful as ever, to say that a fellow guest would be passing my house and would give me a lift in his car up the hill. At 12.30 a honking from the street brought me out all ready for the fray in my lunch-going kit (a slate-gray 'uncrushable' from the Army & Navy Stores) and there, waving from the back of a chauffeur-driven Daimler, was an unidentifiable tallish man (so difficult to recognise people in cars). I opened the rear door and was just climbing in, with a courtly 'How very kind of you', when the words froze on my lips. For there, large as life and twice as menacing, was Boris Karloff, wearing that half smile that usually meant that something extraordinary and excessively disagreeable was about to occur. Although I knew that his real name was William Henry Pratt and that he had been educated at that most reliable of schools, Uppingham, I sank rather gingerly into my seat and kept well into the corner. What might the mute brute not get up to on our brief ride to N.6? Powered by electricity, what shocks might he not apply to sensitive parts? Had he fangs, and if so, where would he sink them?

Horror movies galore came flooding back into my mind. There was the one in which a spider, growing to a height of 100 feet, felt peckish and gobbled up several carloads of people, a real solution to the traffic problem. There was the one featuring a gigantic octopus so expensive to construct that the studio could only afford five tentacles. There was the man-eating plant in the florist's shop which, after munching every begonia in sight, got busy on the florist. Wasn't there some very alarming film in which poor Julie Christie was raped by a computer and, if so, was it acting on its own initiative?

Mr Karloff turned out, I need hardly say, to be entirely charming and easy and not at all averse to discussing his craft. He too treasured favourite moments – the sinister look on the face of Bela Lugosi, a Hungarian actor not given to under-playing, when, as Dracula, he was offered a glass of claret and said silkily 'But I never drink . . . wine'. There was the film based on a short story in which a sea monster falls in love with a lighthouse, a phallic symbol if ever there was one and, what could be handier, fully visible at night-time. There was the film which starred a fifty-foot-tall giantess who kept moaning 'Harry! Harry' and was searching for her husband, wisely absent from home. Mr Karloff told me that enterprising manufacturers produced make-your-own-monster kits, together with glow-in-the-dark plastic vampire fangs.

But all the same, nice as he was, when we got to our destination and he removed his scarf, I took a quick look at the sides of his neck. No electrodes.

On The Move

Though aggrieved travellers by train cannot fail to have noticed and to have applauded Mr Correlli Barnett's stout-hearted efforts in our old friend, 'a popular daily', to get British Rail to see sense over at least two of its many and sad shortcomings it must not be assumed that everything on the travel front is equally bleak. There is a ray of sunshine to be found here and there. A friend of mine, bound for the continent with his car, was allotted a cabin of luxurious comfort (two picture windows, stereo radio, commodious bathing facilities) facing forrard, as we old salts have it, and immediately below the bridge. But it was itself, alas, right above the Bellevue Lounge where a noisy band's insistent musical rhythms made all sleep impossible until 1 a.m.

My friend's subsequent letter of complaint was answered by return of post, bringing profuse apologies, saying that they had now become aware of the menace of the band and announcing that the matter was being looked into. Shortly after, a further letter came, bringing with it fresh apologies and a cheque for £6.50, being the difference between the glamorous double luxi-cabin where my friend had been put by mistake, and the silent and single outside cabin intended for him. The writer politely hoped to have the pleasure of welcoming my friend on board again. He will indeed, for who, after such a civilised exchange and such honesty, not to speak of a cash refund, would ever dream of going elsewhere? But this story has, unfortunately, a sad ending. You were thinking, perhaps, that this was a British boat and that somebody somewhere along the line was at last providing the old-fashioned courtesy that was once such a feature of British travel. Not so, I'm afraid. The company concerned, in every sense, was the DFDS Danish Seaways.

To the normal and everyday perils of travel – lacerations, hijackings, combustion, railway tea, decapitation – a few dangers of a rather more unusual nature must be added and their possibility faced up to, improbable though it may be that the more remarkable of them will ever come one's way. Take, for example, the case (and did I read this in a biography, or was I told it?) of the handsome and distinguished Edwardian lady who, on a journey to London on the old Southern line of blessed memory, found herself cornered by a madman in her first class and corridorless compartment. Enslaved, plainly, by her beauty, he requested her to take all her clothes off and then assisted her to climb up and lie down to rest awhile in the luggage rack where he was the better able to relish visually her charms, half of which must, ipso facto, have been on view at any given moment. Perhaps he was an artist, planning a daring 'problem' picture for the 1906 Royal Academy show ('*Femme nue en voyage*'), not that the exciting prospect of being hung 'on the line' would have brought the lady concerned much comfort at that particular time. However, relief was at hand for her admirer speedily left the train at Clapham Junction and she had just the short run to Waterloo to descend

. . . the risk of being damaged by a runaway mobile lavatory

from the rack, resume her clothing and decide whether or not to tell the police ('It all sounds a bit far-fetched to me. How old are you, madam?').

Well then, among the multitudinous occurrences of an unpleasant sort than can befall us as we progress, with steadily mounting resentment, from the swaddling clothes of babyhood to the winding sheet of thank-God-that's-over, the risk of being damaged by a runaway mobile lavatory cannot, I suppose, rank very high in the probability scale, yet this was a fate visited recently on one of our fellow men. The brief newspaper item reporting it is all too niggardly of just those picturesque details that stamp themselves for ever on the inward eye that is the bliss of solitude but I think we can safely assume that the lavatory, on tow from one joyous comfort area to another, broke loose from its couplings and the tractor that was dragging it, and then achieved a life and momentum of its own, thundered merrily downhill and crashed full tilt into a car that was being driven in the opposite direction. No bones broken, I gather, though the car took quite a pasting and a certain amount of shock was unfortunately sustained by the startled motorist ('It just seemed to come hurtling at me out of nowhere. A *lavatory*, you say?').

But, as all good historians will have realised, the really crucial fact of interest in this bizarre happening is missing, namely, was the lavatory occupied at the time? These mobile contraptions grace our A roads and linger, now here, now there, most welcome amenities which frequently announce (TOILETS AHEAD) their presence in the area, but what steps are taken to ensure that they are empty before they themselves take to the road? Does a sanitary inspector, at about £7,500 p,a, with luncheon vouchers, go through a medium-like knock knock process ('Is there anybody there?') before the green flag can be waved and the contrivance trundles off to bring fresh joy elsewhere? Is there perhaps a helpful HMSO pamphlet laying down the correct procedure (every compartment to be certified as empty on form WC/492/MOB.BOG 83)?

Picture the distress of, say, a sober septuagenarian clergyman, the devout Bishop Merryweather, who has drawn in off the highway in order to satisfy two of the body's most urgent needs – food and the other. Now full of hot dogs and fragrant beverages from the Rest Area's tastefully appointed all-purpose coffee stall, he is enjoying a few thoughtful and sedentary moments behind a firmly locked door. Maybe he is deep in the *Church Times* and lost to the world. Possibly he is meditating next year's Lenten addres-

140

ses. Perhaps he has just dozed off for a space. Suddenly he realises to his horror, after cries from without of 'Back 'er down a bit, Charlie' and sounds of metal on metal, that he and the plastic 'Kosyskwat' seat on which he is perched, together with his snug surroundings, are all on the move and gathering pace. Instinctively muttering a hurried prayer to St Christopher for a safe journey, he must then decide what to do for the best. Flutter paper streamers from the window to attract attention? What about a series of flushings? Would cries of 'I am Bishop Merryweather. Pray allow me to alight' be heard above the noisy hum of wheel on tarmac? Why not prepare your wisest course of action in similar circumstances? Then you've got it all ready, stocked away in memory's bulging treasure-chest under the 'emergency' section.

Many people seem to take travel and its risks quite calmly. At an advanced age, Noël Coward's mother decided to undertake her first journey, and quite a long one, by air. Her friends were anxious about her. Would she not find it, they asked, an alarming experience to be, say, 30,000 feet up over the Atlantic? 'Not a bit', she replied, and added by way of explaining this sang-froid, 'you see, I used to swing very high as a child.'

Stop It At Once

Life at a boys' public school a half century ago was a little short on scheduled enjoyments but at the house, one of 12, that I was in, the housemaster did treat us all, at pleasantly recurring intervals, to sensational moral lectures of a prolonged and fascinating nature. We found them totally electrifying for he was a brilliant speaker, had obviously conscientiously prepared his material, and was quite unaware that, to young people, he was a hilarious figure. Every so often after evening prayers he would stand up and, speaking without notes, let fly. As a new boy, I couldn't always understand why he was so concerned and what had gone wrong. Had somebody, perhaps, said 'Drat' or been rude to Matron or left some gristle or smiled at a boy older or younger (you couldn't smile at a boy in another house at all, and, as I was by nature an inane smiler, I was at constant risk)? But as time went on I began to get the hang of the affair and the gist of the matter and hung upon the housemaster's words, later in the day to be so splendidly mimicked by wags as we disrobed, shrieking, for bed, and cackled ourselves into the Land of Nod.

One of the most memorable pi-jaws, delivered during a power-cut but with flickering candle-light rendering it even more, so to speak, electrifying than usual, began with the striking phrase 'This house is a midden', followed by a dramatic pause while the dimmer boys tried to work out just what a midden was and, if so, what might be the matter with it. On another occasion we were told that 'the trouble' lay neither at the top of the house, where the prefects were, nor at the bottom of the house, but in the very middle of it, and a most pious boy (later a distinguished academic and now high up, and highly respected, in the church), anxiously totting up on the house list, found that out of 63 boys he was the 32nd, precisely in the middle and therefore at the very seat of the bother and deplorably culpable.

Other pleasantly recurring treats, also of a mainly moral kind, were the regular week-end visits to the school of the then Bishop of London, dear old, kindly old, indubitably wonky old Winnington Ingram, much loved by all. He preached, of course, in our chapel on Sunday and, after pronouncing the Blessing at the altar, swung round and dexterously extracted from his billowing canonicals a large gold watch and had a dekko at 'the enemy'. And indeed he was operating on a tight time schedule for as soon as the service was over he repaired to our Natural History Museum which stood close by and there, unsuitably seated amongst pressed grasses and cases of spreadeagled moths and the skeleton of a singularly unattractive horse, he received any boy who cared to call on him solo, and very many did, for a little moral uplift and spiritual encouragement at two minutes flat a head, though the more personable boys could usually count on a few seconds longer. A warm, soft and somewhat clinging handshake concluded the interview. Then he was up and away to a nourishing repast with the headmaster at School House, whence a boy had once written home, 'We had beef for lunch today. The headmaster calved.' And after that, at 2.30, three school prefects appeared to make up a four at tennis with the bishop, a lively player who liked to win and whose wild rushes to the net with a loud screech of 'Mine, partner!' seemed to be in no way slowed down by the fact that he always played in enormous elastic-sided brown boots.

When this delightful cleric was not at Oundle, the newspapers kept us in touch with his doings and activities, one of which was to protest. If there was anything morally unworthy going on and ideal stuff for protesting about, there was the bishop, piping up too. He took against, for some not very clear reason, a play called *The Sacred Flame*. Doubtless the word 'sacred' upset him as the flame part meant love, of course, and the illicit love in the play was far from sacred. So protest he did, to the great profit of the newspapers and even more so of Gladys Cooper, who played the lead, and of Somerset Maugham, who had written it. Boosted by the bishop, the theatre was jammed for months with titillated playgoers and envious theatre managers pressed free seats on him, hoping that he might unearth something and be inspired to protest about *Rose Marie* or *Peter Pan* or *Where the Rainbow Ends*, or *George and Margaret*.

And now, bless me, here he is again after all these years, popping up as fresh as paint and hot on the track of filth, his wails and strictures now resurrected in Edward Bristow's admirable *Vice and Vigilance* (Gill and Macmillan, £12.00), a fine panorama of the various purity movements in Britain. I hadn't fully realised how good the bishop's track record was. In the whole 38 years of his London incumbency, he never once missed a meeting of the Public Morality Council's subcommittee on brothels, the air thick with tch tchs. He kept the Home Secretary on his toes ('I took him in 21 filthy books', and followed them up with a cartload of saucy magazines, light reading that was probably an agreeable change from the official boxes). He spoke out, rather unfairly, against plump ladies in flesh-coloured tights displaying themselves, with not a follicle of pubic hair in sight, in music-hall *tableaux vivants*. In 1934 he announced in the Lords, muddle-headed to the last, that he would like to make a fire of all contraceptives 'and dance round it' (in those brown boots, again).

We remember Macaulay's verdict that there is no spectacle so ridiculous as the British public in one of its periodic fits of morality. Last century's fit was a longish one. There was an agitation to clothe (what with? Bloomers? Jock-straps?) some nude statues in the Strand. Sellers of obscene toothpick cases were ruthlessly tracked down and 'spoken to'. Purity workers, armed with lanterns, lurked at the doors of brothels to identify the customers, subsequently writing up their names on walls. Then the ladies were invited to leave their work awhile and come to church (male salvationists were warned 'never to kneel down with women at midnight meetings, especially behind a pew'). Tea was served, nosegays were handed out by the Bible Flower Mission, and, as soon as dawn broke, there was a group photograph ('Smile, please'), followed by breakfast.

Everybody got very worried and panicky about white-slave traffic and crateloads of drugged and insensible womanhood getting shipped abroad. Abductors, clutching hypodermic syringes, were said to haunt the most unlikely places (Barnet, Banbury, Finsbury Park) waiting to pounce and whizz servant-girls off to Buenos Aires. Beasts in human shape were alleged to rig themselves up as clergymen and, with attractive offers, lure maidens to the capital ('Dear child, you're going to love the British Museum'). The West Ham area was apparently an unexpectedly fruitful supplier of moon-faced girls ripe for Marseilles, and even as late as 1913 the 5,000 girls of London's telephone exchanges were given official warnings to watch out for drugged chocolates. Just the one violet cream or strawberry surprise and everything might go black.

Sweet Mystery of Life

I have always been given to understand that no noise emitted and no sound created on earth ever, theoretically, actually dies away but that its waves wobble on, getting ever fainter and fainter, for all eternity and that if we had a listening apparatus sensitive enough we could tune in to a jumbled cacophony of past sighs sighed, sobs sobbed, yells yelled, shrieks shrieked and, I am afraid, belches belched. How interesting it would be to have recordings of, say, Marie Antoinette putting forward the claims of cake as a nutritional alternative and the musical thud as Mary Queen of Scots (a very nasty and mischievous woman, mark my words) was separated from her head. And so it was that, summoned the other day by the BBC to take part in a performance of 'Any Questions?' on the Isle of Wight, I kept a sharp ear open as we chugged in a splendid Red Funnel ferry up Southampton Water ('A cruise in itself', encourages the ferry brochure) and set out, the trip hardly justifying a Kwell, across the Solent to Cowes. I was listening for the distant reverberation of a cry cried and a wail wailed repeatedly many years ago on that section of the Hampshire coast that by then was visible from our boat. It was 'Boys, boys, I will *not* have this ragging!' Yes indeed, it could come from nobody but a prep school Matron, crackling with starch, fed up with the term and just about to confide over tea to the geography master, for whom she has a secret *tendresse*, that she is at the End of her Tether ('Another bap, Boris?').

My prep school, Stirling Court, stood a bare quarter mile from the pebbly beach and the Solent tides that washed it at such frequent intervals. The school, every bit as bizarre as even the most improbable scholastic establishments of fiction, was in the main village street and hardly a stone's throw from a squat building known as 'The Club', through the unsuitably stained-glass windows of which the outlines of various retired naval gentlemen could be seen most of the day, their sails furled, their long tricks over and their tackle stowed away, exchanging, one

145

assumed, merry yarns with laughing fellow-rovers and drowning in the process a sizeable quantity of booze. As befits naval gentlemen, they had, when seen on the road, rolling gaits but our headmaster, a constant visitor to this cosy haunt, was in no way connected with the navy and owed his own rolling gait to something which came out of a bottle. Watery of eye and purple of face and deaf as a post, it is not easy, even with hindsight, to estimate just exactly how tipsy he was from about midday onwards. A fair verdict would be, I think, 'pretty tipsy'. He was an exceptionally nice and jovial man and we loved him dearly, whisky fumes and all.

Nobody could possibly have been more timid and totally remote than his wife, Mrs Macdonald, the shyest of violets, the merest wallflower at Life's ball. She arranged, presumably, our food, a daily activity which cannot have taken her long. She

We looked at Matron with a new eye

146

engaged, one supposes, the domestics, a giggling batch of warm young plumpnesses who came and went, ruled by an ancient 'working' cook, the dread adjective removing her for ever from polite society, who was to be occasionally seen, a resentful figure in clouds of steam, through a hatch. The Macdonalds' marital union had been once blessed (a clever boy, away at Lancing) and Mrs Macdonald's entire life and interest and devotion now appeared to be centred on a flock of gloomy Buff Orpingtons that tried to scratch a meagre living in a fenced-off (and wisely padlocked) corner of the deplorable and gravelly yard where we larked about ('Boys, boys . . .' etc), fell over and grazed our knees. Occasionally a football would go zooming over the wire and score a pleasing direct hit on a Buff Orpington, a breed of hen with a particularly noisy and satisfactory squawk. Sometimes we increased, accidentally on purpose, don't you know, the shower of balls and there was a general *sauve qui peut* in the chicken world. The balls had to be left there until Mrs Macdonald, basket at the ready, came to undo the padlock, collect her eggs and cluck a greeting to her feathered friends, the birds, hoping for more grain, clucking sycophantically back. It would be charitable to suppose that a fit portion of the Macdonald eggs found its way to us in various tasty culinary preparations though the dishes that graced our table never seemed outstandingly eggy.

I have dwelt deliberately upon this pleasantly rustic, nay almost pastoral and idyllic, scene in order to form a sharp contrast with what follows and thereby give my narrative balance. Life is by no means entirely composed of Buff Orpingtons and from the age of 12 onwards it sometimes seems to have provided nothing but a series of short sharp shocks, physical and otherwise. At that age we none of us had the faintest idea of how babies were constructed or indeed of what a lady's contraptions consisted or looked like. We were soon to find out. By no means all the local naval gentlemen were retired and inactive. Further along the coast and at a place accessible to those of us who were in the sixth form and therefore on Sundays permitted to take 'private walks' as opposed to the deadly crocodiles visited upon the *hoi polloi*, there was a naval rifle range, not in use on Sundays. The steeply sloping butt, backed by a wall, was grass-covered and quite agreeable to roll down if one was in the mood, and in the target area there was a sunken path where, presumably, the markers lurked. There were some locked huts and nautical debris here and there and a trip to this ensemble was more interesting than just plodding along the road. There were also lavatories and into these one

Sunday my friend Williamson, requiring, as we put it, to 'go', disappeared. And not long afterwards there was a loud shriek, though whether of anguish or delight or amazement it was impossible to tell. Hastily joining him, I discovered the cause.

We found ourselves in a picture gallery. No first visit to the Uffizi or Prado could have provided a more astonishing eye-opener. Not an inch of wall space remained unillustrated. Undraped ladies and gentlemen were everywhere at sport, arms and legs in all directions. Occasionally a poet had displayed his gifts ('Here's to the maid who's never afraid') but on the whole the artistic endeavour was in the form of simple line drawings of bold sweep, here and there delicately shaded with black and red chalks, the general theme being that variety is the spice of life. I would like, in my prudish way, to say that we were appalled. Not a bit of it. We were thrilled through and through. No possible doubt remained about what went on. Gooseberry bushes were out and on our return to Stirling Court we looked at Matron with a new eye. Goodness gracious, one thought. Even Mrs Macdonald herself now excited interest and a sense of wonder that she had ever been able to achieve, for the illustrators had aimed high, such strange gymnastics. Talking it all over with Williamson in the days that followed, we found that we shared the same inhibition. It was quite impossible to think of our parents as being in any way connected with these activities. No, no. Parents were different. Perhaps there was something in, and under, gooseberry bushes after all.

And so, while crossing the Solent, I listened, but in vain, for remembered sounds borne on the wind – the hatch doors flying open with a bang and disclosing Monday's unappetising stew, Mr Macdonald's wheezy breathing as we scratched away at an essay ('What I Did in the Hols'), Buff Orpingtons' frenzied squawks and the crunch of Mrs Macdonald's brogues on the gravel, the night-time blubbing of the unbearably home-sick, and Williamson's shriek (he afterwards confessed that it had been one of pure, if one may so call it, excitement) at the discovery of what was what. And did we, you wonder, ever return to the rifle range for a second look? Yes, we did.

Take a Seat

Now that, year by year, an ever increasing percentage of the great British public disloyally abandons the ozone of Frinton and the balmy breezes of Ilfracombe and firmly takes its holidays abroad, there is, I am given to understand, similarly increasing bafflement and bewilderment among novice travellers who have, like poor old Britian, 'gone into Europe' and who discover in their foreign hotel bathroom a useful and watery hygienic contraption to which they are unaccustomed. I refer, of course, to the bidet (say it BEE-DAY, to rhyme with D-Day). One can imagine the anxious family discussion as to what its purpose can possibly be ('Oh look, Tracy wants to float her rubber duck in it!'). It seems to be the right height for squatting down on and is equipped with taps and a plug. A foot-bath perhaps? Obviously it is not intended to cope with anything elaborate such as paper, let alone anything else. Nobody likes to ask anybody outside the family for fear of being thought ignorant and unworldly. After some minutes of non-plussed contemplation, the decision is made to have nothing at all to do with it, except perhaps to use it as an emergency *pot de chambre* for that day when Jason's been on the what's-it for half an hour with Spanish tummy, and Cindy-Lou, with her knickers at risk, has just simply got to 'go'. Bidets in Benidorm must be accepted as one of the many hazards of travel and as unwelcome as that rather nasty foreign tea served in glasses.

The imaginary family of which I write probably does not have easy access to dictionaries but even if it did, the explanatory phrases for bidet do not get one far and primly withhold information as to the prime purpose of the contrivance. I do not run to the O.E.D. but my Chambers's 'Twentieth Century Dictionary' gives for bidet 'a bestridable bath and stand' – not bad at all. My Cassell's French-English section just says 'bath' – hopelessly misleading, and just picture yourself asking a frog chambermaid to prepare you a 'nice hot bidet'. Webster's International Dictionary Vol. I (A–L) gives 'a form of sitz bath', rather feebly transferring the burden of adequate description to German shoulders. And Webster, normally so lavish with its little illustrations of this and that, even with such esoteric subjects as a cardinal's hat, the flower of the gutta-percha tree, grapeshot and a primitive fire-engine, has refused to face the pictorial challenge of the bidet. A plain line drawing of one in use could have been most helpful and would certainly rank in importance with the flower of the gutta-percha tree, which most of us can manage without.

I wonder, incidentally, whether it was left to Webster's illustrator to choose which subjects he got to work on or whether Webster himself led the way ('Today I'd like you to tackle the rotary snowplough, with the weaver bird, if you've got time'). I rather think that only the artist was involved for there is a sort of divine inspiration in some of his work. Who, for example, could resist his likenesses – and here I'm dipping into the M–Z volume, in many ways my favourite – of the herbiverous spotted turtle (such a wise old face), the simple poleaxe, the immensely intricate 'working parts of a motor-car' (an earlyish model, I would say, and possibly a Hupmobile). Everywhere there is visible such a bold attack, such a wide sweep of interest. One moment it is mealy bugs lunching on peaches in somebody's greenhouse, and the next it is the rattlesnake, also on the look-out for something substantial to munch. We flash from a reverberating furnace for extracting lead from something or other (noisy, presumably) on to a rather intimate ventral view of the male squid, and then back to the Murphy Button, apparently a handy device for doing you up inside when the surgeon has been busy undoing you. Wherever you look there is something to catch the eye and hold the interest – panpipes, stilts, a set of wrenches, truffles and a treadmill in full operation with eight merry treaders at work. Very striking too is the illustration of the *trébuchet*, a military engine popular, except with those on the receiving end, in the Middle Ages and capable of lobbing rather large boulders over castle walls as a tactful hint to those inside that it was time to abandon the silly old siege.

Many years ago and during what we called at Cambridge 'the long vac', I went, full of energy, on a walking tour in Brittany with a friend. The sun shone and, having decided never on any account to tramp more than ten miles a day, we merely ambled along, setting out westwards from St Malo and keeping largely to the coast, where there was splendid bathing to be had in deserted coves. The fishy food was excellent and cheap. We became very sunburnt and enjoyed ourselves very much ('What about more lemonade?'). My parents had nobly stumped up the extra cash for the expedition, hoping that it would improve my French, though the opportunities for conversation were few (*'Bonjour'*). At the present time, when young people (and far younger than I then was) just set off into the blue and trustingly hitch-hike themselves vast distances across Europe and Asia, their absences and journeys appear to be taken quite calmly by their parents, who perhaps have little choice in the matter. But I write here of 1929 and our Brittany walking tour was the first occasion in my life when my parents would have no precise idea of where I was. They were kind enough to be anxious and my mother deftly opened up the lining of my jacket, inserted within a five pound note, and sewed it up again. Thus one would have something to fall back on when robbed and tricked and swindled by the rascally frogs, presumably uninterested in my jacket.

At one point we struck inland and found ourselves in Morlaix, an agreeable town of some interest and recently very much in the public eye for you can hardly have failed to spot in the press the sensational announcement that, among other *objets d'art et de vertu* put up for auction there a week or so ago, there was included Marie Antoinette's bidet. An anonymous 'collector' (though whether by that they mean that his whole heart is in bidets and nothing else or whether he likes chinaware in general we are not told) paid the equivalent of £3,900 for it, a paltry sum when you consider where such a unique object has, so to speak, been. But wherever, since the days when French royalty existed and could therefore splash about in it, has it been lurking? Why has this undoubted treasure only recently appeared? Why has it been kept from us? Who has been, as it were, sitting on it?

If only I had been once more in Morlaix and at the auction I would certainly have snapped it up. We do not have bidets in 'Myrtlebank' and this one would be too precious by far to risk ('Ooops!') in any practical way. Instead, I would have tried to make imaginative use of it. Potted up with geraniums, it would make an attractive feast for the eye in a window recess in my dining-room. Or what about using it as a container for the first course at lunch of *les crudités* (I could have done something fancy with bunches of baby carrots)? In the old days it would have done finely as a novel receptacle for the visiting cards that callers left in the hall. And how invaluable at a buffet supper, piled high with strawbugs or, in respectful memory of its owner, cakes. It would make a striking centre-piece for my dining-table, with water-lilies floating in it. Only too easy to draw the guests' attention to it. 'I expect you're wondering about my latest find. Rather a history to it, actually . . .' But too late now, alas. I must wait patiently until it reappears on the market.

The spoilsport BBC, often so firm in discontinuing something that clearly gives the public pleasure (and I wonder yet about Dr Dale and dear Mrs D, both great-grandparents by now I suppose), has never dared, and they'd better not, to lay its hands on either the superb Woman's Hour or the admirable Roy Plomley and his desert island discs. This delightful programme encourages, as you will know, the castaway to take with him to his desert island some treasured possession. I rather doubt whether this is quite the moment for the royal bidet. It might be, to male castaways, too sharp and poignant a reminder of facilities not available amongst the dunes. Washing, I mean of course.

Where the Bee Sucks

I think I may have mentioned before on this page, and possibly to excess in the opinion of flat-dwellers whose horticultural activities are limited to window-boxes, highly pleasing though these are, that the spacious gardens of 'Myrtlebank' are, roughly from January onwards when my witch-hazel bursts into exciting egg-yolk blossom, a riot of colour. I speak of 'gardens' and it may be that you see me in your mind's eye ensconced in a sort of mini-Chatsworth, wondering whether there are enough visitors about to make it worth while to switch on my waters. Not so. I speak of them in the plural merely because the garden is divided by an ancient stone wall, over which japonicas and clematis and roses clamber and intertwine in rich and promiscuous profusion, and this pleasing feature gives me an east garden and a west garden, neither of them very large or grand and in point of fact both of them facing, like stately Myrtlebank itself, due south. The slightest vestige of sun falls full upon us and is gratefully received. The better for residents to enjoy the warmth, there is a small terrace currently ablaze with assorted potted geraniums and scented jasmine. The passion flower, for years such a feast for the eye when festooned round the sitting-room windows and which was thought to have succumbed during that dreadful winter (it even brought a touch of alopecia to my resilient contoneaster, the one which conceals an unsightly drain), is bravely sprouting from the roots.

Any sunshine that tries to reach us during the winter months and which therefore comes at a somewhat oblique angle, is momentarily impeded by some tall trees. They are, I have always understood, Lombardy poplars and they were planted in the first year of the war in the garden of a house at the top of the narrow lane that winds down to me. The house's owner was English but he had a newish and French wife and she, sadly *dépaysée* and a bit of a fish out of water (whatever can that come out as in frog?) in a Devon village where foreigners are, at any time and most of all

during a war, far from acceptable, possibly not too totally delighted with what was then afoot in La Belle France, was considerably
downcast. And so to cheer her up and to remind her happily of
those unique, tree-shaded roads, the kind man planted a row of
poplars.

At all events, we present a peaceful enough scene, you would
think, with 'Myrtlebank' ablaze with sunshine and nestling
quietly among its arums and roses and fuchsias and hibiscus
(they, very mysteriously, *loved* the winter) and snapdragons and
pansies and dahlias and, until quite recently, I would have agreed with you. But now a book has come my way which has told
me, and in almost brutally explicit terms, what is *going on* within
that supposedly peaceful scene. However, in returning once
more to the subject of 'smut', I do so with the clearest of consci-
ences and in an attempt to be helpful and share with others my
recently acquired botanical knowledge, sadly impure though
much of it is. The great thing about 'smut' is to be put on your
guard against it and not to let it come creeping up on you un-
awares. In placing before you my discoveries, I shall have to make
use of words and technical terms that, in ordinary 'smutty' talk,
would be repugnant to me (and, I am sure, to you too, I hastily
add) but on which the scientific nature of our little chat confers a
sort of blessing, if that ecclesiastical word isn't going too far in
view of what follows.

Now then. Starting with the bold statement that 'The plant
kingdom invented sex', the book tells a sorry tale of sexual urges
and gymnastics in the vegetable world that have made me see my
nasturtiums in an entirely new light. The book, and it is a real
winner from the first page to the last, fascinating in content and
with an author who is no slouch with the excellent jokes, is Alec
Bristow's *The Sex Life of Plants*, which Messrs Hutchinson provide
at £5.95. The coloured jacket illustration shows a bee about to
alight upon a flower (harmless enough you might think, but just
you wait), and the frontispiece drawings show a sturdy Stink-
horn or *Phallus impudicus*, in the ready position and the very
image (as far as I can now recall) of the lower midriff portion of a
gentleman in a stimulated state, while above it waits expectantly
a *Clitoria ternatea* (a member, I am told, of the pea family), an
object which speaks, as it were, for itself and if exposed in-
nocently on a newsagent's shelf of magazines would bring
the wretched man instant imprisonment (BENCH RAPS
PORNOGRAPHER. 'DISGUSTING' SAYS MAGISTRATE). There are, you
will be pleased to find, flowers that blush deeply after sexual

154

encounters, so there is hope yet for some show of modesty in the vegetable kingdom.

Splendid Mr Bristow first titillates us with a few remarkable facts (the ordinary garden snail, which plants find useful, is a hermaphrodite and has more than fourteen hundred teeth, arranged on the tongue in 135 rows) and then moves smoothly into top gear with the subject of sexual deception as practised by the Bee Orchid, a delightful-looking species which has a faint sweet scent to it. Its flowers look just like small bees, though whether male or female bees the human eye cannot readily tell. A male bee thinks it can, however. To a virile male bee, out on the rampage and with the whole morning to kill, each little flower looks the very image of a female bee who has forgotten everything that they warned her about in the convent and is yearning to sample Life ('Please show me what to do'). Sensing an easy coupling, the male bee excitedly zooms down onto the flower, mounts it, 'buries himself in its warm brown furry softness and attempts to mate with it. He starts to make a series of short, jerky movements and continues to do so for some time'. But good heavens, what is this? Nothing seems to fit. Nothing jolly happens. What has gone wrong? Thoroughly cross and frustrated, and unaware that in his wild jig-a-jigging he has detached the pollen from the flower's male organ, he buzzes off and tries a more satisfactory sexual union with another bee orchid, transferring in the process the pollen to the flower's moist, sticky concave female surface, rather unfairly known as the stigma. Scientists call this process of false mating with a flower 'pseudocopulation', and one could hardly find an apter description oneself. The whole affair is a most shameful case of teasing and leading on, with nothing but disappointment at the end of it ('Please don't worry me tonight, Walter').

Well then, what about the Bucket Orchid? Here the poor old male bee doesn't even have the excitement of a pseudocopulation. While the flower is, rather like a pub, preparing itself for the day, it fills up its bucket-like receptacle with water from two knobs like taps, and when there is sufficient liquid in it to provide a nice bath for somebody, it lets off a strong and attractive scent, opens up and is ready for business. The male bee, as easily hoodwinked as ever, comes along, drinks a few drops of the scented liquid, becomes drunk and incapable and tumbles headlong into the bucket. 'He lurches around in the water for a while', trying to climb out, and then, on the point of drowning, finds a narrow tunnel through which he can just crawl, knocking

155

off the pollen and sticking it to him as he goes. After further strenuous tunnelling, he escapes and flies off, both perplexed and exhausted, to carry the pollen to another bucket. Were there ever such weird sexual complications?

There is so much else (the book would make a splendid reward for that A Level in Botany). An avocado tree exists which is female in the morning and male in the afternoon (just think of that next time you're sloshing on the vinaigrette). The actual word orchid means, I am afraid, testicle (from its pair of rounded tubers, you know). And in addition to information about their teeth, which I have thoughtfully passed on, there is a lot about the actual bi-sexual mating of snails that I personally am going to try to forget. Mr Bristow closes this episode by merely adding that 'it would be illegal in many human societies.'

Bon appétit

The summer season brings, happily for me, guests to 'Myrtle-bank', old friends from here and there who know the worst, both of the accommodation and of their host. They are normally car-borne, their journeys starting from far afield and culminating in a merry helter-skelter down the M5 motorway in company with the other half million holidaymakers who have decided to head west. However, as they draw nearer to our secluded section of Devon, there is a marked falling-off in the status of the roads. M gives place to A. Dual carriage-ways sheer haughtily off. A gives place to B and there are a lot of 'Give Way' warnings, a road sign which used idiotically to say 'Yield', a word which meant nothing to foreigners and not a great deal to some of us natives. And then even the B designation gives out altogether and the winding and narrow road which leads up from the Teign valley to our little village of Appleton has no status at all although it does appear, if rather faintly, on the larger maps. What is the opposite of helter-skelter? Whatever it is, this would be the wisest method of vehicular procedure to adopt at this stage of the trip. Slow down, engage a lower gear and prepare yourself to encounter sheep, my Cousin Madge off to the village shops, horses, the Bultitudes on their daily walk (Giles in a deer-stalker), assorted dogs and cats, Canon Mountjoy on his way to visit a sick neighbour, and flocks of small children (the soft South Devon air encourages, paradoxically, both sleep and procreation).

My guests usually time their arrival to coincide, after polite screams of 'Oh just *look* at your Albertine!', with a tinkling tea-cup filled with fragrant Earl Grey and flanked by a toasted bun-round if the weather is nippy and I am able to greet them with the relaxed and confident smile of somebody who knows that for the first twenty-four hours at least the main part of the food is all ready and prepared and merely needs to be plunged into my Belling. I own a number of cookery books and the most useful by far are those which contain a chapter headed 'Dishes That Don't

Mind Waiting'. Not for me that last-minute omelette, the timed-to-a-second soufflé, the steamed pudding that needs its water replenishing, the crêpes suzettes and other deliciousnesses that require to be flambé. I go in for the wholesome and more restful stews, Irish or otherwise, the warmed-up apple pie (so odd that pastry will cook itself for just so long and no longer and doesn't at all rebel against gently reheated reappearances), the chicken joints nestling in apple juice and cream, the potato-topped fish pie, the breadcrumbed and fried lamb cutlets that will happily await, for hours if necessary, their moment of nutritional glory. But please let nobody imagine on reading this list that gluttony lurks within my walls. Not a bit of it. It's just the one dish at a time

. . . you can eat stuffed locusts varied with worms and ants

and little else ('Now, who's for cheese?'). I don't, on the other hand, go in at all for slimming dishes. Spuds appear in rich profusion. If something, a stew for example, is all the better for having dumplings nestling in its depths, then dumplings nestle. Fresh garden peas are, and how rightly, anointed with butter. Any soup that should be enriched with cream, gets cream. Why not? Let's live dangerously.

One of my older cookery stand-bys ('A Handy Guide-book for Worried Housekeepers') sets out 365 Seasonable Dinners and although no publication date is given, the fact that sirloin is casually mentioned as being 10d a lb and that each dinner consists of five courses (Green Pea Soup, Boiled Salmon, Veal Cutlets, Strawberry Cream, Cheese Croûtons) must make it, to say the very least of it, pre-war. The book includes interesting medical information ('Digestion Table of Different Foods') about how long the various culinary ingredients require to reside in our stomachs before moving on and down to even more elaborate procedures. The quickest ones to get going ('Hello and goodbye') are rice and tripe which linger for a mere hour. The most prolonged period (5¼ hours) is that required by roast pork. Surprises abound, with boiled cabbage thoroughly above itself and needing 4½ hours if you please, oysters (always said to be so digestible but there for 2⅞ hours) and turnips 3½ hours. You'll want to know about melted butter and tapioca. These work out at 3½ for the former and 2, if you can bear the stuff, for the latter.

Only too well aware of the year-by-year sameness of my *cuisine* and of the fact that guests, half way down the M5, may already be flinching at the thought of my *agneau en fricassée* and my *purée de carottes*, I have been nosing about for novelties and there has come my way *The People's Cook Book* (Macmillan, £5.95), the work of Mlle Huguette Couffignal, translated by James Kardon, and one which deals with 'the staples, delicacies and curiosities from the earth's humble kitchens'. The authoress gives a stern warning of what we are in for – no frills, no pâté, no truffles, no fine cuts of veal, no caviar. Just simple fare 'cooked over open fires from Peru to Pakistan to Polynesia' and providing new conceptions and recipes to set the imagination racing. My summer guests may well be in for something of a surprise. The 'open fires' mentioned are composed, for preference, of camel dung, not easy to obtain locally but I will pay a visit to the supervisor of the Paignton zoo and see what he, or his camels, can manage.

First and foremost, Mlle Couffignal urgently counsels me to procure an iron and oriental cooking utensil called a *wok*. A *wok* is, it seems, absolutely ideal for sautéing and deep frying and boiling. A *wok* is a wide and round-bottomed pot with handles. When perched on a Western stove, a *wok* must, of course, sit on a *wok* ring. Allow no metal cutlery within a mile of your *wok*. It's wooden ware for *woks*. And then, for starters, how about a tasty lunch menu from the Arctic Zone? We kick off with a kind of porridge made from plantain seeds filched from the burrows of field-mice. For our main *plat* it's boiled reindeer (Harrods are bound to have them) with, on the side, predigested lichen from caribou stomachs ('a great delicacy'). And for a salad we have a tossed Siberian seaweed called, I regret to say, fucus. For a pudding, let us seek the hospitality of another land and settle for poe (Polynesian Fruit Balls). Wash the meal down with a pint or two of pulque (cactus beer). Just one thing worries me. How large a haunch of reindeer will I be able to cram into my *wok*? The recipes here say, as so often, 'serves four'. Time will tell.

The paragraph that follows is only, in every sense, for the strongest stomachs (skip if in doubt). There is a Chinese cocktail called Baiga that is made from millet and pigeon droppings. Add water to taste, whizz the whole thing up in your blender and heat gently until fermentation begins. 'Baiga is better', it says, 'if the pigeons have been well fed.' I do see. Well then, there's nothing finer for bucking you up than simmered octopus (but do remember to remove head, eyes, beak and that naughty ink sac). If chancing to be in Tibet, don't forget to ask for fried sheep's lungs, a tremendous local treat, and remember that if your yak butter starts to get runny in the hot weather, a handy larderette can be fashioned from a deceased goat's stomach which will impart an even stronger and richer smell to this essential feature of the best Tibetan tables (yak butter is tip-top in tea and ensures oily globules all over the surface). In Burma you can eat stuffed locusts varied with worms and ants. Never overlook the fact, if you're truly peckish, that grasshoppers are 50% protein. And for a final excitement, much to be recommended is *surprise de termite* (sausages made from squashed termites and rolled up in banana leaves). Serve with airag (fermented mare's milk).

I'm going to find the palm trees on the front at Torquay extremely useful. All palms, they tell us, 'yield sweet sap for palm wine' and are rich in sugar. And another thing: 'the roots can be chewed for dental hygiene'. Palm wine will provide an attractive contrasting flavour for the boiled reindeer and I have written to the Torquay Town Council for permission to fell a dozen or so trees. I cannot see what possible objections they can raise.

Who is Sylvia?

I have sometimes wondered, in one of the increasingly few idle moments that nowadays seem to come my way, what the Christian name of La Belle Dame Sans Merci can have been. She was, as you will know, that lady spotted in the water meadows by a mounted and rather impressionable knight-at-arms. The poet Keats, so helpful in many other ways (and who but he would think of detailing for us the marginal joys of mellow and fruitful but clammily damp Autumn, not to speak of the somewhat limited appeal of both Grecian urns and Melancholy) is silent on this point, so we must search for indications in the text, and few though these may be, they do contain one excellent pointer. Her hair was long, we are told, a wise move to give it, so to speak, its head and just let it rampage for Kirbygrips had yet, in these feudal days, to be invented. She was beautiful and light of foot 'and her eyes were wild', never a very reassuring sign and sadly indicative of instability. She is given to moaning sweetly, a difficult feat, seems to be in the herbal and health food business and inhabits 'an elfin grot', which is perhaps a smallish residence that goes with the job and is therefore a 'tied' grot.

I need hardly remind you of what happens. The knight-at-arms picks her up, in more senses than one, and puts her on his 'pacing steed', presumably seating her in front of him rather than make her cling on as best she can behind for there is a regretful note in his statement that La Belle Dame blocked the view and that he 'saw nothing else all day long', a feeling fully shared by anybody occupying the hind saddle of a tandem bicycle, protected from the wind though he or she may be and spared the onerous tasks of steering, ringing the bell, and finding the way ('Excuse me, is this Watford?'). But La Belle Dame is, I rejoice to remind you, no supine or lifeless passenger. Quite the contrary in fact 'for sideways she would lean', the poet tells us, and obviously with the intention of helping the horse round corners. As to lean when on horseback, now this way now that, can only be the quite instinctive act of a born equestrienne and plainly points to her coming from a hardriding family keen on hunting, the chances are that her name is Diana. I would like to think that, as a tribute to the gifted horsewoman, Miss Prior-Palmer, a name all too seldom mentioned in these pages, La Dame was known to chums as Lucinda, but I fear that, as with Kirbygrips, neither Lucinda nor Prior-Palmer had, as names or persons, yet come off the drawing-board.

Although there is a great deal to be said for Keats, I really do prefer it when poets, after extolling some lady for her beauty or her talents or her wit or her light hand with pastry, let us know exactly who they are talking about and introduce us formally by both their names. It is all very well Lord Tennyson going on as he does, and at really extravagant length (don't be misled by that very small section of the poem reproduced in the anthologies) about Maud (the 'moon-faced darling of all', you recall), but Maud *who*, may one ask? If somebody is invited, nay, positively urged, to come into the garden, one wants to know, before challenging them to a needle game of clock golf, exactly who that somebody is. After all, the vicar may pay a surprise call ('Do I intrude?'), introductions will have to be made, and one doesn't want to look, socially, a clumsy ninny. I rather tend to think that Maud was tacked on to something alliterative such as Maud Merryweather or Maud Majendie or Maud Medlicott. Maud comes from what is obviously a well-heeled and well-born family and therefore Maud Maltravers would have a sort of upper-crust ring to it, besides looking well on the wedding invitation cards ('. . . request the pleasure . . . eldest daughter of Sir Gervase and the Hon. Lady Maltravers . . . and afterwards at Fayreholme Hall . . .'). My dear Essex grandmother was called Maud Marshall but, although she too was moon-faced, she was quite unknown to Tennyson, did not live in a Hall, and can therefore be ruled confidently out.

As a target for Dan Cupid's darts, with the subsequent emotions then freely expressed in partially comprehensible verse, the poet Burns is perhaps more to be pitied than censored. He can be helpful about names on occasion. There was, for example, the fascinating Mary Morrison who, when feeling in the mood, sat at her window dispensing smiles and cheering weary workers on their way home (which in Scottish comes out as 'hame' – anything to be different), a pleasing social amenity which they might try out at Leyland's on a 'no carburettor, no smile' basis. Miss

Morrison, it seems, was mad keen on dancing (those jolly reels, I take it) and was the toast of the town, though the poet wisely suppresses the name of the town. Almost nothing sensible rhymes with Killiecrankie, Auchtermuchty or Spitalburn, and although Cossacks certainly rhymes, more or less, with Trossachs, the presence of wild Russian cavalry in the Highlands gives an unconvincing picture. Apart from our greatly revered and entirely pleasing poet laureate, poets have on the whole prudently avoided place names. There is nothing very poetically rewarding in the actual sound of East Grinstead or Bognor or Edgbaston.

But after that, I am afraid Robert Burns loses his love-sick head entirely and his poems are merely a proliferation of girls' names. There is Jean, described as being, of course, bonnie and residing apparently in West Scotland (one somehow pictures her in Ullapool). There is 'My Bonnie Mary' who lives within shouting distance of Leith pier and whose health is drunk in a wine-filled silver tassie, or cup. There is 'Bonnie Lesley' ('to see her is to love her') who has, we are told, gone 'o'er the Border', possibly to take up a post as a trainee *coiffeuse* in Carlisle. This short poem contains four 'bonnies', an adjective which rather goes to Burns's head. Then there is 'Highland Mary' who allowed herself to be clasped to the poet's bosom (his very words) before dying an early death from some unspecified illness, possibly a severe chill which went to her chest, most of the courting having been done in the open and beneath a hawthorn, never a wise act if the ground is damp. What a lesson for them both!

It is when we come to 'Auld Lang Syne' that maximum bewilderment sets in. It is not perhaps the moment to dwell here on the discomfiture of having, as occasion sometimes demands, to sing the thing with crossed arms (why?) and usually clutching by the hot hand at least one relatively unknown person. The disadvantage to which I here refer is that we haven't an idea to whom the poem is addressed. A childhood chum? Wee Tammy from the manse or braw Jock from the forge? Can it be yet another bonnie lassie (Elspeth from the Co-op)? The addressee appears to be male and the two of them have previously been running about the braes, picking daisies, paddling in burns and now, considerably older, are looking forward to drinking an intoxicant in what will undoubtedly be a public house. But in the last verse, the person addressed is referred to as 'my dear' and eyebrows rise. How acceptable was this phrase at that time? If it had been italicised as 'My *dear*!' we would have known where we were. I am not, frankly, too happy about that daisy picking, hardly a suitable occupation for a truly manly little chap.

Although the poet Longfellow can in some ways be faulted, he is quite splendid about names, and I don't only mean Minne-haha. Though he sometimes takes time off to write a poem about Seaweed or The Arsenal at Springfield or, I am afraid, Nuremberg, when personalities appear we are left in no doubt about who they are – Victor Galbraith (executed by firing squad in mysterious circumstances), Oliver Basselin (a poet based on Normandy), Sir Humphrey Gilbert (a sometimes inexpert navigator with a death-wish) and Gaspar Becerra (failed artist). Even the pop singer at Hiawatha's wedding gets a mention. It is Chibiabos (available for receptions, dances, wigwam parties, etc. Sole agent: Pau-Puk-Keewis. Has own canoe).

On Our Own Heads

When appalling disasters befall nations (the Führer's mad megalomania springs instantly to mind), it is some sort of sorrowful consolation to the survivors to realise that, through blind and supine behaviour (and here our thoughts flash guiltily homewards), they have nobody but themselves to blame. This holds good, and how, for individuals as well. 'Brought the whole thing on myself' is a constant and sadly mournful cry, but a cry uttered without resentment, of human beings who have got themselves into a pickle. But calamities that can in no way be laid at one's door are quite another matter. To be squashed flat in an earthquake would fill what was left of one with furious indignation at the injustice of it all. A nip from a mad dog ('*Down*, Rover!') just isn't fair. To be struck by lightning during the graceful followthrough part of a faultlessly lofted approach shot to the fifth green, with the ball lying as dead as the striker of it, would cause one's angry ghost to haunt the links for ever more, shouting 'Boo!' at tense moments and putting everybody off.

I do not wish in any way to spread gloom and despondency but it is my opinion that every single one of our current British misfortunes and our *dégringolade* (roughly, landslip) into being a laughing-stock among nations ('*Qui pensent-ils qu'ils sont?*') is richly deserved. The causes go back many years but it was perhaps in the Twenties and Thirties that we were to be seen at our weirdest and most wonderful. The poet Wordsworth, such a one for hitting nails on the head ('Our noisy years seem moments in the being of the eternal Silence'), once announced in jocund mood that 'Bliss it was that dawn to be alive, But to be young was very heaven', and although he chanced at the time to be speaking of the French Revolution, 'As It Appeared to Enthusiasts', the general sense of euphoria and the feeling that something very nasty was over at last, will do well for the twenties and for that privileged section that was referred to as 'the ruling classes' (government, peers, church, law and, heaven help us all, 'society'). The war was finished and there would never be another one. Meanwhile, on with the dance. Noisy years indeed.

Looking back now, it is almost impossible to believe that some of the endlessly reported oddities actually took place. A public-school boy attempted to murder the Commissioner of the Metropolitan Police with arsenical chocs ('He got sun-stroke on the playing fields' explained the boy's parents). A Mrs Travers-Smith of Cheyne Gardens, Chelsea, claimed that she was getting spirit messages from Oscar Wilde. The Vicar of All Saints, Cheltenham, suddenly caught fire in the very middle of his sermon: briskly extinguished by the verger, he immediately caught fire again. An Old Etonian, arrested in Vienna for theft, was allowed to send out for his favourite marmalade. Lord Northcliffe, rather losing his hold on things, was found to be living in a small wooden shack on the roof of a house in Carlton Gardens. The first birth took place on the Bakerloo Line, and Bernard Shaw learnt to tango. An old (very old) Rugby boy, had up before the magistrates for swindling, was found to have emergency cyanide capsules concealed beneath his wig. The Maharajah of Patiala's pants were said to cost £200 a time. An Arabian prince escaped from a private asylum in Sussex and was later seen strolling in the Forest of Fontainebleau smartly dressed in female attire. At her christening, Princess Elizabeth yelled so loudly that she had to be liberally dosed with dill-water. Gandhi arrived, bringing with him eighteen bottles of pasteurised goat's milk. Unity Mitford attended various dances with her pet grass-snake, Enid, slung round her neck. Mr Ernest Simpson's 'im-propriety' that enabled Mrs Simpson to get her divorce was with a lady called Buttercup Kennedy. Lord Edward Montagu, off to join the Foreign Legion, decided to open a coffee-stall in Maidenhead instead ('This is just the beginning').

All forms of travel were particularly productive of quaint happenings. The public were aghast to learn of the theft from a train on the Paddington to Oxford run of the manuscript of *Seven Pillars of Wisdom*, though some of course were quite a good bit more aghast than others. At St Pancras there was absolutely no knowing what might not occur. Lady Grimston's diamonds were snatched from her in the refreshment rooms, and the King himself was attacked by a small and club-footed man who struck gamely out at him with his crutch ('Suffering from shell shock, I imagine,' said His Majesty, nobly exonerating his assailant and obviously not noticing the foot). Abroad, the elderly President of France managed to fall out of the presidential train and mooned

Strolling in the Forest of Fontainebleau smartly dressed in female attire

about for quite a time in his pyjamas. The Earl of Craven fell off his yacht at Cowes, hotly followed by Field Marshal Sir Henry Wilson, recently the C.I.G.S. (fished safely out). At the Gare du Nord, Raymond de Trafford was shot by the Countess de Janzé who, on being asked why she did it, murmured 'It is my secret' and was fined the equivalent of 16s. 6d.

Royalty could always be relied upon for memorable moments. The Prince of Wales, dining informally with Mrs Simpson at Bryanston Court, was said to have been fascinated by her raspberry soufflé. His father, however, was considerably less fascinated ('After I am dead, the boy will ruin himself in twelve months'). Queen Mary was here, there and everywhere – at the Chelsea Flower Show and sampling a luscious new strawberry called 'Sir Douglas Haig', attending a performance of *No No Nanette* and lowering her lorgnettes when the bathing-dressed chorus appeared, getting stuck in a lift in Upper Brook Street, being fitted for a gas-mask, trudging tirelessly round the film studios at Denham ('I don't mind steps when I'm interested') and being overturned in her maroon-coloured Daimler and breaking her umbrella ('No fuss. I'm quite all right').

How terribly short one's memory is. Did Mussolini really come over to England in 1922 and, welcomed by cheering crowds at Victoria Station, stay at Claridge's and then dine at Buckingham Palace, where he was reported to be 'in fine fettle'? Did Hitler's nephew, Willie, truly visit his English mother in Highgate in 1937 ('My uncle is a peaceful man') and subsequently announce (in America, wisely) that, in the event of war, he would 'join up immediately for England'? One firm memory does remain. Lady Astor, in Moscow and received by Stalin, rapidly brushed aside formalities and polite chat and got down to important matters ('When will you stop killing people?').

In the pre-war years, anything might happen. A conveyor-belt was installed at Chatsworth which transported the ducal soup the 109 yards from kitchens to dining-room at a speed of 7 m.p.h. Princess Margaret made her first trip by Underground and found herself sitting next to a charlady from Muswell Hill. The Duke of Manchester popped some jewellery that didn't actually belong to him and was himself popped into Wormwood Scrubs for a month or so. Disgraced MP Horatio Bottomley appeared in non-stop variety at the Windmill Theatre (assorted anecdotes and chestnuts, followed by a heart attack). The French-born Begum Aga Khan declared that Hitler was the most attractive man she had ever met (newspaper heading: BY GUM, BEGUM!).

168

The source of all these fascinating facts is Andrew Barrow's *Gossip, 1920–1970* (Hamish Hamilton, £10.00), a handsomely produced and lavishly illustrated cornucopia of delights.

Behind the Scenes

Nobody in their youth can ever have been a keener amateur actor than hopelessly stage-struck I. Year after year, audiences sighed and flinched and fidgeted and looked at their watches as I strode the boards and boomed disastrously away in plays by Barrie and Shaw and Sheridan, to name the most reputable. Nor was that all. In lighter vein, I was perfectly ready to rig up in pierrot costume and, a revolting spectacle, dispense and ruin musical items by Coward and Farjeon. Nothing and nobody was safe from me, though it was not until I was nineteen that I was able to get my hands, so to speak, on Shakespeare and mess him about. This was at Cambridge when the Marlowe Society, a distinguished band of skilled and seasoned performers, part dons and part undergraduates, decided to do Henry IV Part II, a work with which I was unfamiliar, and kindly allotted to me the role of the Earl of Surrey.

Hastening to a copy of the text and searching eagerly through the Dramatis Personae, I instantly spied the name of the Earl of Surrey, proudly listed with two other earls, Westmorland and Warwick, described as being 'Of the King's Party', and clearly a person of note. It was with considerable excitement, and wondering whether my talents would be equal to the strain of this exacting part, that I turned the pages, seeking my big speeches, my moments of high drama, my sword fights and, with luck, my eventual death in the King's cause with somebody saying, over my dead body and as the curtain fell, 'What courteous nobility was here! Sleep on, sweet Sir, and take thy well-won rest.' Or something. Great heavens, I could hear the cheers already.

I do not know how recently you have seen or read Henry IV Part II but just in case it hasn't come your way in the last month or so, let me tell you that you have to be pretty nippy even to spot the Earl of Surrey. There is no chance at all of actually hearing him utter for he does not speak. The Bard has provided for him no words. Moody silence is his. His entrance is certainly saved excitingly up, with the audience on the alert for him, until the very beginning of Act III when, accompanied by the Earl of Warwick, he enters a room in the Palace of Westminster and finds there the night-gowned King who has wound up a long and self-indulgent soliloquy about the great benefits of sleep by saying that he himself cannot sleep and then adding a line that one has heard before somewhere – 'Uneasy lies the head that wears a crown'. Meanwhile, Surrey just stands there and, with him speechless, pushful Warwick greets the King with 'Many good morrows to your majesty!', and when the insomniac old dodderer replies 'Is it good morrow, lords?', Warwick presses on with a time check – ' 'Tis one o'clock and past'.

This seemed to me to be an immensely unfair distribution of lines and I refused to put up with it. The undergraduate cast to play the Earl of Warwick was an agreeable friend of mine in Trinity. Hurrying speedily round to his rooms in the Great Court, I found him – it was about eleven a.m. – drinking, as was his sensible mid-morning custom, a healing glass of cointreau and deciding not to attend any lectures that day or, indeed, any day. He kindly poured me out a generous measure (oh we went the pace in those days, I can tell you) and, in the heady fumes of the delicious liqueur, he sportingly agreed to see things my way and to allow me to say his line, ' 'Tis one o'clock, and past.' I gave it, both in rehearsal and performance, everything I'd got. The experience gained from fourteen years of amateur acting was lavished upon it. Sometimes I said it boldly. Sometimes I said it wistfully. Sometimes I said it reproachfully, implying that we had been kept up long after our bedtime. The line never actually got a round of applause but it kept audiences, I felt, on their toes, wondering among themselves when it was going to be that nice Earl of Surrey's turn to speak again.

At one of our matinées of the play there was for all of us a great thrill. A very famous actress, Irene Vanbrugh, later, and in 1941, to be Dame Irene and who had, I think, a young relative in the cast, came to a performance and sat, splendidly visible to all, in the third row. It was my day for saying my line boldly and I directed it straight at her. ' 'Tis one o'clock, and past', I trumpeted, every word a jewel of clarity and superb elocution. It could, I felt, hardly fail to impress her and when, some years later, she wrote her agreeable autobiography, *To Tell My Story*, I hurried to it to see what she had to say about that memorable afternoon. There would, surely, be a reference to the performance and to my line, perhaps in diary form ('Thursday. Rain morning. Lunched hotel and went afternoon to production by Cambridge Marlowe Society. Was much struck by Earl of Surrey'). But no mention of the matinée or me was made. Odd.

And then, in the strange way that things happen, four years later I had the good fortune to meet Miss Vanbrugh. She was appearing, in a very starry cast, at the Palace Theatre under the banner of C. B. Cochran and in the successful American comedy, *Dinner At Eight* by George Kaufman and Edna Ferber and in which she played Millicent Jordan, the hardboiled New York hostess whose snobbish social aspirations (Lord and Lady Fernecliffe are invited to dine but fail to turn up) assemble round her table a rum collection of ill-assorted guests, every one of them worried and unhappy in some way or other. The piece was in eleven scenes and had to be played at great speed, with lines thrown away or trampled on, a relatively recent technique to which American actors and actresses were at that time more accustomed than English ones, and least of all Miss Vanbrugh. She had been brought up in the excellent stage tradition of clear, measured speech. You waited to speak until the other person had stopped speaking. She had created the part of Gwendolen in *The Importance of Being Earnest,* Pinero wrote plays specially for her, and she was the original Lady Mary in *The Admirable Crichton.* Search the plays of Wilde and Pinero as you may, there are no lines that can either be hurried or thrown away. The same applies to Barrie, apart from a few that one would wish, for other reasons, excised. Miss Vanbrugh was at the time 61 years old, a latish age for learning new tricks and so the engagement was in the nature of a challenge.

I had become very friendly with a delightful niece-by-marriage of the Vanbrughs and together we saw the play (and a splendid theatrical evening it made) and afterwards went round to see and congratulate Miss Vanbrugh. Playing against the grain every inch of the way (tough and nasty women were never her line), she had given a remarkable performance, and in her dressing-room she displayed all the charm and tact and modesty that made her so much loved. And she had, heaven knows, needed them when trying to cope with Mr Kaufman and Miss Ferber, both of them formidable characters who had come over to London after having triumphantly launched the piece in New York and who plainly did not regard the somewhat solid and statuesque Miss Vanbrugh as ideal casting. She told us that when, on one occasion at rehearsal when he was attempting to get extra pace on the dialogue, she had said 'You know, Mr Kaufman, you are asking me to speak quicker than I can think', his reply had been a crisp one: 'Then don't think'.

Meanwhile Miss Ferber, snugly housed at Claridge's, was, as she tells us in her autobiography, disenchanted with everything. There were fogs, she disliked London, she hated the Palace Theatre and, when her spirits were at their nadir, news came to her from rehearsals that Miss Vanbrugh was planning, in the last scene of the second act, to wear 'pink lace lounging pyjamas'. She then, to cap all, caught influenza and was somewhat startled to hear her English maid announcing this misfortune to Mr Kaufman down the telephone wires and in the accepted phrase of the time, 'Miss Ferber's very queer today'. The phrase held a different meaning for Mr Kaufman who, the soul of loyalty, is said to have replied, 'Not when you really know her'.

A Woman Wronged

I have recently been refreshing my old and, for many things, sieve-like memory about Branwell Brontë, brother of those three semi-weird sisters and only son of the Reverend Patrick, originally of Drumballyroney, County Down, and formerly called Brunty but, on arrival in England and Cambridge, adapting it to Brontë, Nelson having been created Duke of Brontë in 1799 and the new name bearing with it therefore a distinction not possessed by Brunty. I had not forgotten, and indeed who could, Branwell's fondness for the bottle (such an especially exciting treat for the locals when the pastor's son keeps measuring his tipsy length in the bar parlour of the 'Black Bull') and that he was for a time railway booking-clerk at a small Yorkshire station where it seems probable that sad and boozy muddles were made and that passengers, seeking to travel humbly down the branch line to visit a sick aunt, found themselves whizzing, complete with luncheon-basket, in a first class smoker to Manchester.

But I had not remembered what must be, apart from his unusually gifted female relations and his artistic ability (portrait painter), his chief claim to fame – an embidexterity which fills me with envy and which allowed him to write simultaneously two quite different letters, one with the right hand and one with the left, thus halving the time required for correspondence. Cheers greeted this parlour trick when performed in the 'Black Bull' before the whisky had taken its relentless toll and, with a clatter, poor old Branwell disappeared yet again beneath the table. Eventually the railway company installed in its booking office a rather less risky employee and Branwell's briefish interval of usefulness to the travelling public was at end end.

Branwell also wrote, and how deafening must have been the endless and noisy scratching of pens in that Haworth Parsonage. Not a shy author and sheltering conveniently behind a pseudonym (Captain John Flower, MP), both prose and poetry came easily to him and be sent the former to Mr Blackwood of

174

Blackwood's Magazine, who refused it, and the latter to William Wordsworth, who didn't answer. Meanwhile his sister Charlotte, not yet known to the public but with *Jane Eyre* just round the corner, was sending her poems to the Poet Laureate, Robert Southey, who certainly answered and a fine wet blanket he turned out to be, damping her enthusiasms with talk of literary 'daydreams . . . inducing a distempered state of mind . . . literature cannot be the business of a woman's life, and it ought not to be.' Although it must be said in Southey's favour that Charlotte's gifts were not for poetry, the grumpy and discouraging letter does him little credit and makes one doubtful once more about the whole subject of poetry and poets and the very limited amount of interesting information they seem willing to pass on to those of us who like to know where we are. I recently complained in these pages about the absence of full names in even the best poets (Keats, Burns, etc.) and now complain again about certain other facets of this rather flowery and pretentious way of arranging words and expressing emotions.

Take, for instance, Southey himself. I shall come in a moment to the deplorable vanities revealed in his poem 'The Scholar', elsewhere called 'His Books' and 'My Days Among The Dead', few poems being less deserving of three assorted titles, but first let us examine what is possibly his best known poem, featured in Palgrave but cold-shouldered in the Oxford Book of English Verse, and called 'After Blenheim' and which begins, as you'll recollect, by telling us that 'It was a summer evening' and that 'Old Kaspar's work was done.' For those of us who instantly cry 'What work?', there is an answer. Here at least Southey bestirs himself to let us know that old Kaspar is an ancient ploughman who ploughs up, unwisely one would have thought, the late battlefield, and also comes upon distressful remains when digging his garden.

Although there are some who claim that Blenheim is in Oxfordshire, it is in fact in Germany, no great distance from the town of Ulm and extremely adjacent to the river Danube, every bit as un-blue and disappointing here as it is further down. Kaspar, presumably a widower for no apple-cheeked *Frau* is discovered immersed in *Sauerkraut* and yelling 'Supper's up', is now taking it easy outside his cottage door but is not alone, for 'by him sported on the green his little grandchild Wilhelmine.' Apart from the deep horror and shame for a girl of having to press down Life's pathway called Wilhelmine, where, you may well enquire, were the child's parents? If they had gone on a shopping expedition to

Ulm ('Don't forget the Frankfurters!') we should have been informed. If they were an athletic and fun-loving couple and were decorously splashing each other in the Danube prior to practising their crawls, pray come out with the details.

But it is in the latter part of the poem that Southey's general feebleness is so sadly apparent. You'll remember that Wilhelmine's little brother, Peterkin, comes running up clutching a disused skull and is, naturally, full of questions about the battle of Blenheim, to which Old Kaspar supplies the thinnest of answers, never attempting for one moment to explain what our very own Duke of Marlborough was doing so far away from home and impertinently fighting a war on territory that did not even belong to the enemies he was up against. Here was both Southey's and Kaspar's chance for a general review of world power and strategy at the time, and they completely muffed it, the latter merely mumbling that ' 'twas a famous victory', which we knew already, and doubtless shoving aside with his foot two or three more Frog skulls that had popped up while he was preparing the winter cabbage bed. And the poem could have closed on a cheering horticultural and 'it's an ill wind' note by drawing attention to the very fine beetroot crops gathered in the district over the next decade or two.

The poet's excellent opinion of himself is there for all to see and regret in the aforesaid 'The Scholar', the opening line of which runs 'My days among the Dead are past', past here meaning passed. Although this bold statement may give the impression to some that, his poems having understandably failed to sell ('remaindered' at a bob a time), Southey has gone into the more financially reliable undertaking business, this is not so. He is referring to the great minds and writers of the past (Shakespeare, Aristotle, Voltaire – you name them) with whom he is in daily and dusty confab in the library and hence Palgrave's title of 'The Scholar'. He certainly expresses thanks to these great minds, even though there is a sort of girlish gush in the words selected ('My cheeks have often been bedew'd with tears of thoughtful gratitude'), but one senses that he really regards them as equals and indeed the poem ends with a smug reference to his own assumed immortality and to the fact that, when he is dead and gone, it is among these same illustrious Dead that 'I with them shall travel on through all Futurity'. Not for him a seat on the clouds with humble ploughmen, even one called Kaspar, but stimulating chin-wags over coffee and biscuits with Homer and Mozart.

176

I very much doubt this. There is nothing that I can find in the works of Southey that convinces one that he would be regarded as in any way an acceptable figure up aloft and given a cheery welcome ('Do take a pew'). I can see him trying to thrust his way into a bridge four with Ben Jonson, Pepys and Isaac Watts. I picture him at lunch attempting to edge into a seat well above the salt and alongside Virgil and Aeschylus ('Close up, for God's sake. Here comes Southey!'). Although in heaven all will be perfection, one will surely be allowed a few little simple human failings such as mild irritation ('Go away. Southey!'). And what, may I ask, will happen when, scuttling round a corner and in vigorous pursuit ('I say, hold on a moment') of the Venerable Bede, he finds himself face to face with Charlotte Brontë? Forgiveness, I feel sure, on her part, but what on his? Blushes and confusion and abject apologies? One can only hope so.

Now it Can Be Told

Truth will, as people never tire of telling each other, out, a reassurance of considerable comfort to me for there is no greater lover of the truth than I. Indeed, if anybody ever claims to have discovered a deliberate 'fib' in these pages, they are at liberty to discuss the circumstance with my lawyers. By 'these pages' I mean, I hurry to point out, only those pages that have housed my weekly column (about the other richly fact-strewn pages I wouldn't presume to speak). And lovers of the truth the whole world over will have had, in recent years, cause for rejoicing at the discovery that almost nothing is as one thought it was – that Lee Harvey Oswald did not assassinate President Kennedy, that the tragic death of Martin Luther King was quite otherwise than as reported, and now we find that Hess is not Hess at all but somebody quite else. Encouraged by these revelations to speak out myself, let me say that for many years now, worried by, in paintings, the size of Napoleon's hips, I have had a theory that Napoleon was in fact killed in mid-career, probably at the Battle of Austerlitz, and that the wily French generals, anxious to maintain at its highest pitch the superb morale of the splendid army, hurriedly brought over from Corsica Napoleon's little-known twin sister, Hortense, who took over from then on. I need hardly say that the frog authorities whom I approached with the perfectly reasonable request to be allowed to open up Napoleon's tomb and, with competent medical assistance, examine the skeletal remains, adopted a very stuffy and unprogressive attitude. Like the sadly anglophobic General de Gaulle, the word 'Non!' came all too easily to their *bouches*.

It is not, however, about Napoleon that I wish this week to write but, emboldened as I am by the recent and above-stated setting straight of records, about an even more impressive person and one rather nearer home. I can only, of course, be referring to Queen Victoria and to that famous 'missing' week at Osborne in the summer of 1860 that has worried historians for so long, that week in which, and quite inexplicably, she wrote no letters, initialled no government papers, and received no ministers. That week in which she, and it is the right word for it, vanished completely. My family has long known the true facts, for my great aunt Eleanor was very closely involved, not because she was in any way in court circles but merely because she happened to live at Cowes, was fond of walking, and owned a dog (Tinker). Although sworn to silence, she left a detailed, if rather poorly written, account of the astounding incident, which I here condense though the original will, on my death, be offered to Her Majesty for the Windsor archives. Meanwhile any bona fide historian is welcome to examine it.

It was on the very last day of that famous missing week and on June 17th that Eleanor, who must then have been in her very early twenties, set out with her dog from East Cowes for a walk after tea. Although the week had been cold and rainy, it was, she records, a nice bright day and she had had no hesitation in leaving both her macintosh and galoshes at home. She chose, who knows what strange spirit guiding her, a path that ran along the coast and which, at one point, skirted a small bay popular

Victoria rushed into the royal bedroom

with swimmers. Bathing in those days was, of course, performed, in the case of ladies particularly, from bathing-machines, mobile wheeled cabins that were pushed or dragged, sometimes by donkeys, into three or four feet of water, thus allowing the occupant to disrobe in private and to remain modestly concealed until actually descending the steps and lowering her body into the briny. Queen Victoria herself was known to enjoy a dip and delighted to walk alone from the grounds of Osborne House to this very bay where a bathing-machine attendant, an elderly woman called Mrs Grimshaw, saw to the royal needs.

Beyond the line of bathing-machines, pulled up well above the high tide mark for the week's poor weather had discouraged their use, there stood a row of beach huts and Tinker, running on ahead, was scratching and whining in a frenzied manner at the door of one of these huts (Eleanor, doubtless in an attempt to increase the suspense of her narrative, breaks off here to tell us that it was painted a rather nasty lime green and was called 'Kosikot'). Drawing nearer, she was horrified to hear from the interior a series of muffled wails and groans and, pushing open the door, was appalled to see, dressed in nothing but an extremely crumpled magenta bathing-dress, the bound and gagged figure of Queen Victoria (Eleanor, a doggy person if ever there was one, adds at this point 'What an excitement for Tinker!'). Even had she not recognised the monarch, the first phrase that sprang to the ungagged royal lips ('The perpetrator of this monstrous outrage must be *very severely punished*') would have told all. When Eleanor, in a hurried aside, says that not only was the perpetrator never punished but was instead given a very large sum of money, and by the Queen herself, your astonishment will be as great as mine when I first read this amazing document.

A hasty, stumbling rush up the hill to Osborne House followed ('Tinker greatly enjoyed his extra little walkie'), with a shivering and dishevelled queen clutching Eleanor's arm and alternately sobbing her heart out and choking with rage. And on the terrace, whom should they find but Prince Albert, cool as a cucumber, who just said casually 'So glad you're better, liebchen. I didn't know you were coming down. Had a good swim?' Coming down? Better? What could this mean? Who then was, or had been, upstairs? Supported by Eleanor, Victoria rushed to the first floor and into the royal bedroom, to find, in her place in the royal double bed and in the royal nightdress, a bewigged person who certainly looked remarkably like her but who in point of fact turned out to be the dumpy manager of the Ventnor branch of Barclay's Bank and whose name was Gideon Willoughby.

A word, or two, by way of explanation will make all clear (the Queen, not daring to question her ladies in waiting and thereby spread the scandal further, clung like a leech to Eleanor, partly as a confidante and partly to prevent her enlivening tea-parties in Cowes, both East and West, with the thrilling details). Eleanor therefore didn't miss a thing. It emerged that Willoughby ('Giddy' to friends), a wonky transvestite who had had a great success at parties with lifelike imitations of his sovereign, had conceived a violent passion for Albert and his manly charms and had dreamt up a desperate plan. Informed by the bribed Grimshaw that Her Majesty was expected at the bathing-machine on June 10th, Willoughby instructed this treacherous woman to keep away and, taking her place and waiting until the Queen had changed into magenta beach wear (for he was going to need her clothes), he pounced on her, tied her up and gagged her, placed her in 'Kosikot', put on her dress and bonnet and, returning to Osborne, pleaded a migraine and gave it out that absolutely nobody, nobody but Albert that is, was to come near. He then retired to the royal bed and awaited results in a state of pleasurable anticipation.

Frightful thoughts tortured poor Victoria. Why had Albert noticed nothing? Or, worse, had he? What sort of conversations had gone on between Albert and his new bride? *What else*, if anything, had gone on? What if Albert, reaching out for a section that was normally soft had encountered a section that was the opposite? Could it be that Albert had far from disliked this change of scenery? One heard such stories these days. The crazed woman, mad with jealousy, settled half a million pounds on her marital replacement provided that he instantly left the country (he speedily got into tremendous trouble in Rome). And Albert? Dead almost within a year of typhoid and heart-broken, it was said, over the Prince of Wales' many shortcomings. Hm! I wonder. Heart-broken certainly, but for whom?

And so now, when anybody tells me that Hitler is alive and, after a sex-change, is doing sterling work on the assembly line (hubs section) of British Leyland, I shall believe every word.